To Barbara and Mike
from Alastair with love;
July 2020.

The Golfing Life of Jock Kirkcaldy

Frank Crowe

Designed and Edited by Alastair Allanach

Grosvenor House
Publishing Limited

This book is published by
Grosvenor House Publishing Ltd
Link House
140 The Broadway, Tolworth, Surrey, KT6 7HT.
www.grosvenorhousepublishing.co.uk

A CIP record for this book
is available from the British Library

All proceeds to Heavy Sound CIC
www.heavysoundcic.co.uk

ISBN 978-1-78623-616-6

This book is dedicated to
Lady Margaret Scott, past and present.

Lady Margaret Scott
British Ladies Amateur
Champion 1893, 1894, and 1895.

Contents

Acknowledgements

Gary Player, Foreword
Malcolm (Moly) McMillan – Foreword
Ian Cowie, Photography
Rob Anderson, Illustrations
(Lady) Margaret Scott, Patience
The Author and Editor would like to thank the staff of Grosvenor House Publishing for their valuable and expert assistance in the preparation of this book
Moira Campbell, Bank of Scotland Private Banking - *Financial help!*

Credits

Golf Books

Teach Yourself Golf, Dr J C Jessop, The English Universities Press Ltd, 1964
A Round of Golf with Tommy Armour, Tommy Armour, The Lyons Press, 1996
Into the Bear Pit, Mark James, Virgin Books 2000
How to Play Golf by Harry Vardon, Methuen, 1912
Golf by Henry Longhurst, J.M. Dent & Sons first Edition 1937
The Guinness Guide to Golf Equipment, David Graham, Guinness Publishing 1993
Power Golf, Ben Hogan, Originally A S Barnes & Company, 1948, also Simon and Schuster 2010
My Swing by Henry Cotton, Country Life Ltd 1952

The Picture Story of the Golf Game by Henry Cotton, World Distributors Ltd, 1965

The Principles of Golf, by M. J. Astle, W R Chambers 1923

All About Golf: How to Improve Your Game by Bert Seymour, Ward, Lock & Co 1924

Knave of Clubs, Eric Brown, Stanley Paul 1961

Bobby Locke on Golf, Bobby Locke, Country Life Ltd, 1953

Bedrock Principles of golf, W W Lowe, Collins 1937

Essentials of Golf by Abe Mitchell, Hodder and Stoughton 1927

A New Way to Better Golf by Alex J Morrison, Heinemann 1932

How to Play Golf by Harry Vardon, Methuen 1912

The Way to Golf by Harry Weetman, Ward, Lock & Co Ltd 1953

Golf from Two Sides by Roger and Joyce Wethered, Longmans Green 1925

Golf Begins at 50, Gary Player, Simon and Schuster, New York, 1981

Gary Player's Golf Clinic, Beaverbrook Newspapers Ltd 1973 to 1980/ DBI books Inc. 1981

Photographs

From many sources, for which many thanks

Bibliography

Wikipedia – many entries, cross-checked with many other sources

Artwork

Argent Brierley photographs. Copied from a variety of sources. No copyright infringement is intended.

Foreword

Gary Player

I have at least two things in common with the author. We both have a passion for all things golf, and we both have degrees in Law from Dundee University in Scotland. The author's was a starting point for his legal career, while mine was awarded in 1999, for services to golf. I had already made my name in the golfing world!

I'm pleased to see the publication of a golf book which encompasses a number of golf-related components – short stories, reminiscences and golf equipment among them.

    I'm pleased that the game which has given me so much pleasure and fulfilment (and of course occasional frustration) can be shared by so many others through the medium of print.

This book contains a fine balance of fiction and non-fiction. The author's obvious obsession with (and patently love of) golf is amply described in his accounts of his golf books and clubs.

As the author of many books, on a variety of topics, including golf, fitness, golf/life balance, my favourite golf courses and others, I know the passion I have for sharing my experiences and knowledge, and so feel I am well qualified to fill the role of golf book critic. While I am aware that P G Wodehouse wrote several humorous accounts of fictional golf life, I'm sure that the combination of items in this publication are at least unusual if not unique.

I'm also pleased to note that donations will be made to charity from the distribution of book, which I understand will have a limited print run. I can only encourage those of you who are acquire the volume to give generously to the nominated charity. Most of those who can afford to play this magnificent game can afford a little extra to support those less fortunate than yourself.

Gary Player recently changed his golf club affiliation to PXG (Parsons Xtreme Golf), and in line with the nature of this book, we think it appropriate to list the golf clubs now in his bag, and show a photograph of him with his clubs.

What's in Gary's bag?

- PXG 0811 X GEN2 Driver, 9°
- PXG 0341 X GEN2 Fairway Woods, 15° and 18°
- PXG 0317 X GEN2 Hybrids, 22° and 25°
- PXG 0311 XF Xtreme Dark GEN2 Irons, 6-PW
- PXG 0311 T 100% Milled Xtreme Dark Wedges, 50° Sugar Daddy, 56° Sugar Daddy, and 60° Zulu
- PXG GEN2 Brandon Putter, Black, Plumber's Neck

Gary Player with his PXG clubs, July 2019

Foreword

Moly McMillan

I eventually met Frank some months after I joined the board of Apex (Scotland), a charity providing rehabilitation support for offenders. Frank was also a board member, but had missed my first few meetings, probably due to some jury trial; I had started to wonder whether Sheriff Crowe was in fact a fictional character, created to fulfill some government criteria of the charity.

So it was with a little suspicion, I must admit, that I sized Frank up upon finally being introduced to him. I, like most people brought up in a Scottish tenement, had visions of a judge being rather highbrow and posh, with "plum fully in mouth".

Frank didn't fit my prejudiced view at all - albeit it took a little while for me to make that conclusion, since at board meetings he didn't say very much, if fact in the first meeting I can't recall him saying anything at all! Over time I realised that the Wisdom of Solomon takes far more listening skills than talking skills - I suppose that's what Judges' do – they observe, they listen...only when fully considered do they "judge".

I'm not sure whether this is a compliment or not, but it's how I feel; you would never guess that Frank Crowe was a Judge, from his demeanor, appearance, accent, attitudes or what he speaks about. He speaks about things like Guinness, football, pie and chips, politics and of course.......golf! I realised Frank and I shared a joint love in golf shops - only, I loved going to golf shops, whereas Frank loved being a golf shop.

After playing a number of times with Frank, I observed that he never seemed to have the same golf clubs with him twice. Now, we've all played with people who every season buy the latest driver, in the forlorn hope their game will be unlocked. But with Frank, the clubs seemed to get older each time; "look at these latest shafts Moly, they're the 'bees knees'". "Aren't they hickory Frank?". Thankfully Frank adheres to the rules of golf, not surprising for an administrator of the law - for him the most important in the R&A's book is Rule 4.1.b(1) covering the Limit of 14 Clubs. Goodness knows how many clubs Frank might consider appropriate – "one to cover every shot" might have a more literal meaning than intended.

Isn't it a joy to listen to someone who has a passion for something that in of itself is rather senseless and none more so than with collecting things – Frank collects golf clubs, golf books and golf stories. This book is actually in a way a collection of collections. My challenge to the reader, is to try and work out what is fact and what is fiction, because although the book may appear to be 6 fictional short stories and 6 'autobiographical' essays about golfing matters various, I think there are strands of truth (A BIG WORD) that run throughout. Think Terry Gilliam's fantasy 'Brazil' meets Sunday Post Sports Classified Ads (Western Isles Edition). Conjure that up, and, well….conjure that up.

Amidst the short stories there are some wonderful characters, expertly illustrated by Rob Anderson. But one can't help wondering who actually is "The Scratch

Man", "The Boys Champion", "The Dealmaker" and "The Thirties Man". Are they Frank's father, his alter ego or his obsession? Oh yes, you can't help but conclude that Frank may actually be a trifle obsessed with Golf – and so it is with very many Scots, as we feel collectively that we, "the people", own the game of golf, not the R&A, and most definitely not the Honourable Company of Edinburgh Golfers.

Is Golf a religion? Well, by modern definitions, if "consumerism is a new religion", then for the Scots I dare say that Golf could be too, as it often requires deep faith and believe in one's self on the golf course – perhaps that once in a lifetime 1-iron sweetspot find, does actually require divine intervention. Like going to Church on Sunday, you might lose your faith, but there's a strong draw back. If golf is a Scottish religion, then what kind of golfer would the Saviour be?

It has been an immense pleasure of mine to recommend the reading of this book through this foreword, and to make a final summing up of Frank Crowe and his book. Golf is about many things, not just about the score you make; it's about humility, friendship, obsession and, perhaps, a religious zeal for the game.

I have the only conclusion possible: Frank Crowe, you are a true "Scratch Man".

Introduction

I have been a keen but rubbish golfer for over 50 years. Sadly after a few early years learning the basics of the game and about twenty years as a club member, golf has had to take third place to family and work, and has been confined to holidays, odd days off and evening rounds in the summer.

These drawbacks have not stopped me from reading, watching and dreaming about this wonderful game. The transferable skill I took from golf was that you should never compare yourself to anyone else in life but to do your best in playing the course as it lies, and in the environment of the moment.

It is a game you need to practise regularly and play as often as you can to keep up your skills, as the ball rarely lies flat on the fairway in an inviting position ready to hit as if on the tee.

My busiest times golfing were when I was a member of a Winter league in my first job, and played Gullane No 3 each month together with regular office competitions and outings throughout the season. Later on when my daughters were newly born and after rising about 6 30 to assist with the morning feed, I could get a round of golf in before 9 am when the family woke up. Once on holiday I played 54 holes in a day over Lossiemouth's fine courses, two rounds by 10 30 am before the family became restless and one in the evening after the kids were tucked up in bed. I played consistently better when a club member entering a few competitions and having regular games with a low handicap friend.

I had hoped to spend more time golfing when I became a sheriff but learning a new job and commuting 600 miles a week were not conducive to this. I also thought I would have time to dictate some golf stories during court adjournments and I had heard other shrieval colleagues used this down time to compose pibroch tunes on a chanter, and wore out the carpets in their chambers marching up and down in this enterprise.

About twenty years ago, I did get as far as composing a list of short story titles so that I could pick up the threads at a later date. Sadly I mislaid this note but could remember enough to get the first three stories going. In that regard tribute must go to Alastair Allanach. At one of our regular lunches at the Outsider restaurant in George IV Bridge, Edinburgh, when he spoke of writing about golf courses for travel magazines, I confided that I would like to write some golf short stories for a golf magazine of a type I seem to recall in issues of Golf Digest about 40 years ago. Nowadays with new golfing equipment and apparel coming out each month, a few tips and articles about the pros, there is little space for whimsy and imagination.

Alastair challenged me to write a story and soon rising to this task I wrote several over the Christmas period, and with his suggestions and advice I was able to draw my ramblings into what is hopefully a more coherent form. There are a few fictional short stories, with some inter-connection, a few scribblings about my passion for golf memorabilia, books and clubs, and some encounters I have had while playing. This is a book for average golfers everywhere. I was never very good at the game and preferred social to competitive golf, but every now and again there would be, somehow, a flash of something out of the ordinary, inexplicable and such that I rarely was able to emulate the feat, but sufficient for a competitive soul to be beaten by a duffer. I did relish those few moments!

I made many friends on the course and built up friendships with others as we battled the Scottish elements. Most of all I liked playing on my own. Just like running, when you get your second wind into a rhythm and have to concentrate on your breathing, so too with golf; once you begin to play steadily and become focussed on the task, all cares evaporate; you have time to enjoy the view, study the topography, gauge the wind speed and direction, and keep an eye on the clouds to avoid getting soaked.

It is definitely a walk enhanced by these sensibilities.

Editor and Author during one of their many editorial lunches held in the Outsider Restaurant, George IV Bridge, Edinburgh

Close Encounter of
a Golfing Kind

Chapter 1

It was my father who arranged for me to become a member of Silverfield Club; he was more of a cricket man himself. At an early age he must have seen that I had no skill at football, hated rugby and generally did not get team sports.

We played a few games of putting together and then he sent me for lessons with the local pro, an elderly man in a bunnet who took classes each Saturday morning and gave us kids 5 minutes each and told us to practise the rest of the time. By 13 I had quite a good swing and enjoyed the freedom of the course on quiet days. I lost a lot of balls in the fierce rough and my inability to clear the fearsome carries at certain of the tees, but the occasional good shot or short-hole par kept me going.

By contrast my next door neighbour in Kirkcaldy was Derek Small, a few years older than me but already an accomplished golfer whose feats as a teenager were the stuff of legend to my friends and I at Balwearie Golf club. Derek had a successful career as a golf professional, playing on the European Tour, teaching in the Bahamas and becoming club professional at Dunbar and Gifford. In retrospect he was a subliminal inspiration for what could be possible.

A move to Edinburgh in my teens made it more difficult to play golf, my parents unable to afford to put me into a private club, and while I loved some of the municipal courses, 5 hours on your own behind some slow foursomes stretched one's patience.

I didn't play much at University either but when I started work as a graduate in a large multi-disciplinary office I found active golf and curling sections where I enjoyed the company of older colleagues and in retrospect these contacts helped me progress up the management ladder.

One of the guys at work – Mike, was a friend of my Father and together they must have hatched a plan to bring me into a proper club. An introductory game over Silverfield led to a loss of 6 balls in the penal rough and whin bushes, but a par four courtesy of 2 drawing 5 irons between the whins and two putts on tricky sloping green got me hooked. My move coincided with the start of cuts in local authority services which led among other things to fairways only being cut once a fortnight. You got a few lush lies but some stinkers from the centre of the fairway!

*"The more I practice, the luckier I get." -
Gary Player*

Through the golf club's curling section I got to know Silverfield's 'Old Contemptibles', a club within the club which offered a game each Sunday morning, other fixtures permitting. All you had to do was pitch up about 7 45 am for an 8 o'clock start with the captain setting us off in 4's, 3's and the odd two. Not being mathematically inclined I marvelled at how quickly he fixed up the games whether 13, 17 or 11 turned up - prime numbers were a speciality. It didn't matter if you promised to be there the next day after a Saturday medal or re-appeared after a few weeks' absence, the old men, many of whom were ex- forces were a kindly bunch and understanding that a young man like me might not always be able to get up on a Sunday after a late night.

I did enjoy getting up early to pay golf on freshly switched greens to remove the morning dew but leaving a little moisture to stop the ball disappearing off the green. What a contrast to the slick surfaces the last group of a Major have. They have to to contend with worn, crowned holes, spike marks and the ghastly dings left when players lean on their putters to remove the ball from the hole.

Chapter 2

However after a few years my wild social life curtailed my early morning golf and indeed much golf at all. I was in a crowd of young lawyers who liked to drink and party and go weekends away to exotic cities or have outings to racetracks. Needless to say there were a number of young women who found our group at least superficially attractive. My favourite was Julie, and for a while it looked like she and I would become engaged but by the time I started to think about rings and the like she went off with my then best friend Tam. I couldn't face going to their whirlwind wedding and must have become a bit depressed, withdrew from the group and stepped up the drink.

My father, an ex- detective, was first to note the change in my habits and appearance - a certain flabbiness had crept in as well as a blotchy face and bad temper. "What about your golf?" he said one day after a Sunday lunch where I had drained the bottle of Sauternes (they knew nothing about wine) instead of restricting myself to a glass like my temperate parents. "Well, I haven't felt like playing recently and was thinking of packing in my membership. Take last year for instance - each round I played must have cost over £100."

Depression fell over the meal, however after Mum's excellent Eve's pudding and custard Dad said "If you promise to play regularly like you did most weekends I'll pay next year's subscription."

So the following weekend, shamed into it, I had a quiet Saturday evening and went off to bed after Match of the Day football on TV and no drink. I had heard muttering in my rare visits to the club that the Old Contemptibles were disappointed about my no-shows and had heard rumours about my drinking. Their disappointment almost seemed on a par to the original Old Contemptibles, the British Expeditionary Force of the First World War and maybe thought like their German foes I had come to dislike them.

Anyway next day was a beautiful late August morning and I awoke at 6 am and by 6 45 had teed off, first of the day with no one in sight. Soon I was up at the top of the course on Corstorphine Hill looking over Edinburgh, with the Firth of Forth and Fife to the North, the Pentland Hills to the South and in the east the Bass Rock and Law Hill signalling North Berwick with Muirfield, Gullane, Kilspindie and Luffness to name but a few golf courses lying in between.

Although my play was naturally a bit rusty after a long lay-off with slicing, rather than my trusty fade making good scoring impossible, I was enjoying myself. By the time the Old Contemptibles had started out I was on the back 9 and out of their sight although they must have noticed my trusty British Racing Green MGB GT with silver Minilite wheels tucked away in the car park. That feeling of being on my own on the course at the top of the hill was greatly exhilarating and I resolved to go to the driving range 3 nights a week. I re-subscribed to the golfing channels on TV and looked forward to my early starts on the course each weekend, and I even fixed up a few solo outings to Eyemouth and Goswick in Northumberland.

As winter drew in I found myself starting just before the old Contemptibles but they just gave me a cheery wave. I had bumped into one of them, old Bill, at the supermarket one week and told him I'd hit the bevvy but had taken the pledge and was practising to get my swing back before I felt good enough to join them (and risk my 50p first nine, 50p back nine, pound the game and 10p for birdies which were their staple stakes); theirs was a hard school!

Chapter 3

That was my routine that winter and only severe weather, when the course was shut in early January, interrupted my progress. It was on an indifferent Sunday morning in March when few other golfers had ventured out. I had hit a shot on to the green at the short downhill 10th at one of the more remote parts of the course when I was surprised by another golfer appearing from nowhere round the hedge which protected golfers teeing off at the 16th from errant tee shots on the hole I was playing.

"Do you mind if I join you?" said the man in an odd accent which I could not place; "I'm Deimos, a temporary member. I've been practising on the range up the hill but fancy a few holes before I pick up my car. That was a superb shot you just hit." Only the most churlish could refuse such an offer and while I had been in my own zone these past few months

DEIMOS

9

getting my game into shape, maybe it was time to try it against an opponent playing at the same time with the same weather conditions – and being a Scot, this was my weather. "OK" I said. "Do you mind if I try for my birdie?" "Of course not" said my new friend and he tended the flag as I lined up a putt of about 15-18 feet. It was my favourite positon, slightly uphill, right to left where I could bend my blade on to the ball – none of this rigid modern stuff. I had a 'gate' type putting swing where hopefully ball and club were lined up correctly only at the millisecond of impact. Anyway I put my best swing on it and the ball curved in to the centre of the cup with some authority. "Well done!" Deimos said with a thin smile but with warm eyes. He shook my hand again and I noticed he was wearing golf gloves on each hand. He noticed my glance immediately and said "ah yes your Scottish weather means I need 2 gloves," and we both laughed. He didn't seem a natural joker but appeared an affable companion.

"Your honour" said Deimos as we walked on to the 11th tee. Flushed with my recent success in front of a witness my drive was not my best over the blind summit, and I knew I had sliced it into the rough or perhaps the cherry trees.

Deimos pulled out his driver and without any practice swing hit an effortless shot straight over the hill. "Good shot!" I shouted. Deimos was well up the fairway at this tricky par 4 and well placed to stop a mid- iron on the plateau green. By contrast I had a ball-below-the-feet shot with my 4-wood albeit from a better than expected lie in the rough. I took my time and flexed my knees to get down on the shot and allowed for the inevitable fade from such a lie. I hit a cracker and with a fortuitous bounce to the left of the green my ball jumped right following the terrain and rolled up to the flag. "That was an amazing recovery" replied my opponent. He put his bag down and after selecting an iron, hit his ball high and straight on to the green about 20 feet way, On the green Deimos's putt spun out of the hole after what seemed a perfectly stuck putt. I holed my 6 footer and was one up.

"What's your handicap?" I asked my new friend. "Scratch, I suppose," replied Deimos, in an almost absent minded fashion. The next hole was a shortish, fairly easy par 4 which Deimos won with a four after I took on the flag with my new confidence and dumped my approach shot into the intervening greenside bunker. The next hole, a short par 3 was halved in 3's after I scrambled an up and down after over-clubbing and putting my ball in rough to the right rear of the green. Deimos by comparison was a model of consistency with a safe 9 iron to the centre of the green and two putts, the latter being a tap in.

The 14th is a tricky par 5 with an Eisenhower tree about 175 yards out which the top guys clear with a high draw off the tee. Deimos hit a brave straight shot at the tree and his ball somehow sailed between the branches and bounded down the fairway in good position. I faded my ball past the tree and although not so long as Deimos was well-placed. It was a fairly close cropped lie but I took out my Tour Spoon, an elderly Taylor Made metal wood with a small head and hit one of my best shots with it. I had picked this club up in a bargain bin at a Golf Shop in St Andrews and was told by the owner it had belonged to a touring pro but he couldn't play it consistently and had discarded it. If truth be told I couldn't play this club consistently either but now and again it delivered the goods (or was that me)?

Deimos's wood shot to the green was high and straight but by the time we reached our balls I saw to my joy mine had ventured on to the putting surface whereas his ball was short and he had to pitch over a tricky bank. It was an awkward lie, downhill with the ball above the feet, the sort of shot Silverfield regulars cope with through years of trial and error. It was no surprise that Deimos duffed his chip leaving ball to trickle down the bank towards the green but disappointingly rest on the collar of grass surrounding the putting surface. Deimos appeared to hesitate before selecting his putter and hit the shot as before without a practice swing, and failed to factor in the dew on the collar of grass. His ball rolled towards the hole but only covered half the anticipated distance. Deimos remained expressionless but his body language was eloquent of the shock of a major miscalculation. I had two for the hole from 30 feet and although the second putt was 4-5 feet away I slotted it in to go back to one up.

The 15th has its subtleties too and although Deimos outdrove me by 30 yards with another effortlessly straight shot he had hit it too far to get a view of the green for his second shot and missed the green. I had a decent view of the green and faded a 5 iron into the wind and on to the front right corner of the green. Deimos had a poor chip from an indifferent lie and once again I capitalised on his failure to make par and went two up.

I knew how to play the 16th and let my opponent out drive me then hit a lazy 6 iron to the top of the ridge short of the green and let the ball run down to the flag placed in the back third of the green. I had noted the flag's position just before teeing off on the previous hole. By contrast Deimos hit an excellent pitching wedge but failed to allow for the tailwind and couldn't appreciate how the trees near the hole funnelled the breeze over the green. The result was that his ball bounced off the back of the green and lay in rough on the rear slope less than 25 feet from the out-of-bounds.

Instead of taking a 6 or 8 iron as I would have done on the upslope, Deimos ballooned a pitching wedge and still had 15 feet to go to make par. His putt was on line but too strong and hit the rear of the cup flew in the air but stayed out. My 15 footer was fairly straight on what was one of the easier greens and I confidently stroked it in.

"Well played!" exclaimed Deimos with what seemed genuine emotion and shook my hand with his gloved one. "What do you play off?" "it used to be 6 on a good day" I replied. "You've excelled yourself today. I must dash off, I have a meeting but I hope to play you again." And with a wave and no parting glance Deimos strode off towards the Practice Area car park and was lost to view.

The 17th was an easy uphill par 4 but despite my blistering run of golf from the 10th my head was buzzing with the game with my new friend and an indifferent 6 resulted. The 18th, always a tricky finish only produced a bogey 5; my opponent had inspired and intrigued me.

Chapter 4

I mulled over my game with Deimos for days afterwards. He seemed like a robotic par machine and hit mostly perfect shots but lacked guile, though he could not know any of Silverfield's idiosyncrasies and subtleties.

I had almost forgotten about him when I went out for an early round during the weekend of the Edinburgh Spring April holiday weekend. A combination of lots of members being away on a weekend break and pretty foul weather meant I was almost the only one brave enough to venture out. I did however notice a small group of the Old Contemptibles playing 2 and 3 ball games, and I reckoned they would turn back and not go out into the country for the second 9.

I had sliced a poor 4 iron off the medal tee at the 10th when just as before Deimos appeared from behind the tall hedge. "Terrible weather isn't it? Could I join you for a few holes like the last time?" I had all but decided I was going to cut in after the 10th and play the last 3 but my curiosity got the better of me and I agreed to play. I hit the better drive over the hill at the 11th this time and we set off. The last time I had been somewhat transfixed by Deimos that I could barely remember what sort of golf clubs he had but this time I immediately noticed the silver pencil bag he carried and the bronze coloured irons which protruding from it.

As before Deimos approached his ball, selected a club and executed his shot almost in a single movement. The whole process must have taken 2 seconds compared to the 2 minutes allowed in tournament golf to enter the striking zone, clear negative thoughts, throw grass in the air, narrow the selection down to a single club, check yardage charts, loosen the sweaty polo shirt from the shoulders, grip and re-grip the club several times, have innumerable practice swings before hitting and hoping it will match the inner trajectory and finish you have loaded into your brain (which may have been wildly optimistic).

Deimos was on the green whereas I yanked my approach shot to the flag and missed the elevated green and rolled away downhill to the right into light rough. Despite making the green with my pitch Deimos made his par after shaving the hole from 15 feet and I couldn't match it. He finally had a birdie at the next hole (the short par 4 12th) to my par and seemed in line for a hat trick after his tee shot at the short 13th landed softly 4 feet from the flag and below the hole on the tricky left to right sloping green. I took my time over a 9 iron and took the tight line over the guarding bunkers to land on the left front of the green; the ball rolled up close but was a tricky 3 ½ feet above the flag leaving one of those curly putts that often embarrass. I was playing an old blade putter in those days and lined the ball up just beyond the sweet spot which I had marked in pencil on the top edge of the face. This allowed me to swing smoothly and feather the ball into the cup. "Great putt! I didn't think that was possible," exclaimed Deimos. It must have unsettled him as his much easier putt rolled past the hole and I had stopped the rot.

It was my honour at the long 14th and with a slight following right-to-left breeze I set up for a slight draw and hit one of my best drives which curled past the Eisenhower tree and ran on as it smoothly hit the fairway. Deimos tried not to look concerned but when he played a similar shot to the last time the wind bent it slightly, it hit the tree and ricocheted out of bounds. The hole was lost and we were all square. I held my drive at the 15th into the right to left breeze and it landed in light rough to the left with an excellent view of the green and to my mind in the perfect spot. Deimos's straighter longer tee shot once again left him with a blind approach.

I noticed he walked up the left side of the fairway to my right to view the green then tacked across to his ball, took out a 7 iron and hit a perfectly decent shot into the green. The pin was cut in the front right corner and Deimos has clearly thought he could land the ball just short of the green and let the ball roll up to the flag which was no more than 10 feet from the front edge. I knew this was near the lowest part of the course and was not surprised when the ball landed on the false ground short of the green and stopped dead. By contrast I was able to play a three-quarter pitch and run with a 6 iron and bounce the ball off higher ground to the right of the green and then the ball rolled on to the front of the green 6 feet from the flag.

Deimos's chip was a bit clumsy and although his putt looked like it was going to fall into the hole, the softer slower green held the ball back and denied it the last half roll into the cup. I stroked my putt in with the authority of an early morning golfer allowing for the moisture and was now in the lead.

We halved the 16th in 4's and then proceeded to the 17th. "This will have to be my last hole," said Deimos. It was an uphill shortish par 4 which was driveable from the winter tee; today however we were teeing off no more than 10 yards in front of the medal tee about 90 yards back.

I faded my tee shot into the rough but only had a wedge or 9 iron to go over the right hand bunker as the pin was well set back, meaning the trap was not in play if a decent shot was executed. Deimos was straight up the middle but once again he had a poor view of the second shot he had to play. I hit a wedge out of a reasonable lie and allowing for the ball to run, watched it land beyond the bunker and roll up towards the flag. Deimos made the green but overshot the hole and was left to putt back from the rear fringe. He had the par in the bag 2 quick putts later, leaving me with 2 shots for a win. I took my time over a 12 foot putt which had a touch of right to left and although it was meant to be a lag up close to the hole it dropped in as I had planned.

"That was superb!" said Deimos generously. He offered a gloved hand which I shook and doffed his cap when I did so. His hair was peculiar, but I only got a flash of it.

"I shall be moving away soon," said my opponent. "I may not manage another game with you, but you have such talent and local knowledge." I would like you to have these clubs." I was quite taken aback as the silver bag was thrust in my hands and at that he turned, gave me a cheery wave and a nod and strode off towards the practice car park. As he turned to go I saw a mark down the side of his neck, about 6 inches long, like a gill, but it was just a flash and with so many emotions going on in my head, not least my best golf for a long time this didn't register at the time.

I looked down at this strange collection of clubs and when I looked up Deimos had gone. After examining the clubs for a few minutes, marvelling at the quality of the materials and workmanship I walked in the direction of the car park as I had not heard any car. I reached the enclosed practice ground a few minutes later but the car park was empty. The assistant pro was giving a lesson to a lady member and I walked up to them and asked if they had seen a tall, thin man pass by but they hadn't. "Been buying new clubs?" asked Dave the young assistant. "No I've just been given them by this guy I've just beat over 7 holes," I replied. "What kind are they?" replied Dave advancing towards me. "Och, some foreign make, probably Japanese," I responded. "Sorry to interrupt your lesson," I nodded to the lady and turned and walked off briskly. I had seen enough of the clubs that they were not the sort of things you wanted people to examine closely.

Chapter 5

The bag felt light as I walked back to my own clubs but individually the clubs felt solid. I reached my caddy car and pulled my bag away from the 17th green, walked through the gates to the 18th fairway but made no attempt to walk back to the tee or indeed stick a ball down and play the rest of the hole as we often did if a match had been settled on the 17th. I walked down the left rough as quickly as I could and on reaching the car park briskly opened the tailgate of the MG dropped the silver bag within, covered it with my own stuff and jumped into my car with my spikes still on. An Old Contemptible, now too old for active service on the course but all dressed up for the bar to open sidled over. "Hello Jock, how are you?" Gerry was an old blether and I was not in the mood. "I'm not feeling well, I think I have picked up a bug and just want to get home," I replied and drove off as briskly as someone in such a condition might drive.

Fortunately no one was hovering about near my flat, the church mob had already set off for the Sunday service and out of respect, the gardeners had not started grass cutting and clipping hedges.

I quickly rummaged in the boot of my car, extracted the silver bag, left my own gear and rushed into the house, closing and snibbing the door behind me. I grabbed a beer and sat down to examine my hoard. There were

12 clubs in all – a driver with a loft of about 10 degrees, a 4 wood with a loft of about 15/16 degrees and a low profile head, 9 irons which I later discovered had lofts of 20, 25, 30, 35, 40, 45 50, 55 and 60 degrees, and a plain blade putter similar to mine except it felt weighted internally with just a tad of weight in the toe.

Each club had a bronze finish and the head seemed to segue into the shaft and then into the grip in a seamless fashion. It was as though each had been manufactured from some strange metal composite which could morph from a solid head, to a flexible but firm shaft and then transform into a warm comforting leather-like material with which to grip the club. Each one was like a piece of art and yet simply functional. There were tiny hieroglyphics on each club but I could not decipher them. I must have spent the best part of the day looking at them and admiring the smooth finish, the bag was made of a fine sliver mesh-like cloth but appeared light and water proof and was comfortable to carry via a single strap which was fairly thin and rigid but was comfortable on the shoulder.

I desperately wanted to try the clubs but they looked so *avant garde*, nay futuristic, that I didn't want to go out with them. I meant to say all this occurred about 30 years ago when the Ping square grooves controversy was at its height and keen golfers were alert to any strange looking clubs and would have wanted to examine the faces of these magnificent implements. My mind worked overtime handling the clubs and bag. Inside a pocket I found a single ball and tee and a spare pair of golf gloves which seemed about my size but had fairly long fingers. The material was leather-like but of synthetic construction. The gloves were comfortable to wear and had areas in the palms and fingers where the material was particularly grippy at points matching the perfect grip that would hold the club. My mind was racing and I lay down on the bed. Next thing I woke up, it was 5 am and I appeared to have fallen asleep holding the bag and clubs in both arms!

Chapter 6

I couldn't contain myself but secured the set in a locked cupboard, put the key on my house and car key ring and waited until the next dull miserable midweek evening and took them to the driving range where I knew it would be quiet. To the surprise of the assistant at the till I selected an unloved booth some distance away from the ones being used by two particularly keen young amateur golfers. The results were sensational; I was able to hit long straight shots with each club about 1-2 clubs further than my own set. It was possible to manipulate the ball slightly but not much hence Deimos's steady golf.

Part of me wanted to go public, tell this amazing story, display these fantastic clubs and make them available for expert scrutiny. The other part of me felt I would look a bit daft even if I had the clubs to provide some credence to the story of my games with my mysterious opponent.

So I have kept these clubs close to me in the ensuing 30 years. I have practised with them occasionally and played the odd round on a clear, quiet course on my own. I had a narrow escape once when a young man strode across the fairway when he saw a club glinting in the sun. He grabbed one of the clubs and examined it with increasing incredulity. Fortunately my pre-arranged Plan B came into play and when he asked about them I said I only played with them in practice rounds as I was not sure if they were legal. I confided that they had been made by NASA who were flushed with success in the early 1970s after the Moon landing and Alan Shepherd's famous 6 iron shot. I said I had been given a set which were disposed of when further moon expeditions were cancelled.

In the intervening years I have reflected, made notes and tried to sketch what I saw. Maybe this is the paranoia born out of years of over analysis but every now and again I go to a nearby bank vault where I have them locked away and take out a club or two from the set to admire them. It was like having a stolen Old Master. I could only admire in secret occasionally but never share my joy and mystery with anyone else.

What have I concluded? Well it took me some time to find out that Deimos is the name of one of Mars' two moons. I checked with our golf club and no such person was ever taken on as a temporary member at that time. I realise he or they must have watched me and saw me as a lone creature of habit playing reasonable golf that they could take on. Deimos's golf was very consistent, a bit robotic but well executed yet like the Japanese golf driving range pro who was chucked out of the Open Championship in the wake of the Maurice Flitcroft scandal. He had swung impeccably on the tee but had never played off grass and his score had soared. How someone could develop an excellent swing and ball striking capacity on a driving range but be hopeless out of the course must have been peculiar. While the putter was beautiful too I realised it had no loft on it and was hopeless except when playing on a freshly cropped green. It was OK at home on the carpet.

As far as I could recollect Deimos's clubs for our first round were some proprietary bunch of "game improvement" irons which were OK to play but a bit clunky in tight lies and from the rough. By the second game some work had obviously been done by his team to create this master set. Maybe they knew I'd be discreet. Anyway, as golf club manufacturers strive to tell us each year, they have bent the laws of physics and their driver is 15 yards longer than the opposition. I occasionally glance at their puny offerings as I stride through the golf shop to the driving range; they've still got a long way to go!

THE BOYS' CHAMPION
by Argent Brierley

25 Years Ago

Suddenly there was a horrible crashing sound like I had never heard before or since. I still feel it. Fifteen years later I was rear-ended in my modestly sized courtesy car by an elderly lady in her pink Cadillac Eldorado. I was playing later that week in the Las Vegas Open. It was nothing like this.

I had been out with my best pal Jimmy Gibb; we had eaten pasta at a local Italian Restaurant in his home town of Falkirk and had planned our two-pronged campaign to secure playing cards for the European PGA golf tour. Although he didn't have far to walk home I offered him a lift in my old blue Morris Minor which I had parked outside the eatery facing the oncoming traffic.

As well as the horrendous noise that followed, I have re-lived the minutiae of that evening many times since, both in dreams and flashbacks. We had such a laugh at the meal. I was always keen and enthusiastic and Jimmy was laid back, interjecting my stream of upbeat chatter with well-timed but kindly put-downs and comments.

We were due to travel to the South of Spain in a few days' time and each of us had things to do before then, so this had been the final planning meeting together before we met at the airport. I had some sponsorship, Jimmy had some winnings from the local Tartan Tour and savings from a part-time job and we were going to room together and rent a small car when we reached Spain so as to keep our costs down.

I unlocked the driver's door with the worn key; the lock was worn too and any implement would have afforded entry. I climbed into the driver's seat and reached across to open the passenger door for Jimmy – no central locking in those days. When I thought back later there was a rushing sound from an oncoming car. I was unsighted as I was engaged in starting my car, then came the impact, a glancing blow from another car which took my passenger door off and my friend out of my sight. I was showered with safety glass; the passenger window dissolved into chunks which although not jagged and supposedly safe left me with numerous superficial cuts which I only noticed some time after.

I had been thrown back in my seat, was dazed and shocked and it seemed like several minutes before I got out of my car. A crowd had already gathered including waiters who had just served us. There was no sign of the other car which had been driven off. I forced my way through shouting "he's my mate!" Jimmy was lying awkwardly on his back on top of the door which had been wrenched off my car. He was motionless, eyes closed and blood running down his face and body where his clothes had been torn in the impact and crucially his left leg lay at an impossible angle. I felt sick and powerless. I started shouting "Jimmy" until someone, I think it was a girl from the restaurant, led me away and back into the place where we had been happily enjoying ourselves a short time before.

I wasn't allowed to see Jimmy the next day – he had been in theatre most of the night and continued to be sedated afterwards. I was numb and just hung about the hospital waiting for news. Jimmy had no family, so I acted as next-of-kin. Eventually the following evening I was allowed in to see him briefly. The doctor and a nurse told me that normally they wouldn't have let anyone see Jimmy at this time but he had recovered consciousness and shortly after had asked to see me and had been insistent about it. It was then they delivered the hammer blow that Jimmy had lost his left leg, and an amputation had been performed above the knee. Their timing was perfect, no doubt perfected over the years like a good golf swing. I was dumbstruck and was led into a dimly lit room where Jimmy lay, his bedding was like a vast cocoon over his legs. There were tubes leading out to bags and drips leading into his arms. His normally weather-beaten face was ashen but his eyes, though tired had a steeliness about him.

"Jimmy, we can let you see your friend for a few minutes but you need to get some sleep to rest and recover" said the doctor. "Hi Argie," croaked Jimmy. "I wanted to see you to tell you not to worry – I'm fucked but I'll be worse if you don't fly out tomorrow and qualify for the Tour. It'll be a skoosh cos I won't be playing so you've got an extra chance – don't blow it, yah posh bastard!"

"Jimmy, I can't leave you like this!" "Yes you can, I'm finished!" he said like the squaddie in one of our Commando comics who insisted on being left behind wounded with a clip of ammo in his Sten gun, and a last cigarette in the corner of his mouth. "I'll see you sometime, but you've got to go!" "I think that's enough. It's not good to get too excited just now, Jimmy," said the nurse. With that I was led out of the ward with barely time to shout "Take care! I'll keep you posted! We'll be playing again soon!"

The next 10 days were a bit of a blur. My Mum and Dad got me organised and took me to the airport. Somehow I got to Spain, collected the Ford Escort we had booked and got to the two star hotel which I found was miles from the tournament venue for the final stage of qualifying for a place on the European Tour.

I just had time for one practice round and needless to say had a shaky start in the tournament proper. I was in danger of being eliminated at the halfway stage but despite the nightmares I had each night and flashbacks at quiet times on the course I began to put some scores together thanks to Jimmy's words in my ear.

With 18 holes to go of this 6 round marathon I had clawed myself up to 10th place and after some hard self-motivational talking to myself before setting out on the final round I felt composed, focussed and determined to succeed. That's all very well sometimes but that day the ball soared high and straight as I swept the shots round the links and stroked the putts with ease, close to or into the hole. An amazing 61 shots put me well into the lead when I finished and none of the groups who played behind me by dint of finishing ahead of me after the previous round could come near to matching my score and I took the winner's cheque with 2 shots to spare over my nearest rival.

Present Day

I hadn't been in Scotland for a while – not since playing in the Open at St Andrews 18 months previously. I didn't like coming back much nowadays after my dream marriage to Miss Scotland had failed and my parents had split up and then hooked up with ghastly partners. I had however agreed to open a new sports section in Jenner's department store in Edinburgh and was flying up from London for the event and began thinking of Jimmy. I was 48 and in sight of rebirth on the Senior Tour. I hadn't won for a year or two on the regular tours, still golf had been good to me; I had been Rookie of the Year when I started playing on the European Tour and after winning 2 events I took my call up to the Ryder Cup in my stride with the arrogance of youth. I kept improving each year and then got married, but within a few years it had all fallen apart. I had been playing more on the US Tour and seeing less of my new wife who chose to remain at home with our daughter. I 'got lonely' on tour and soon succumbed to the charms of the girls who follow the players. Before I knew where I was I was divorced, taken to the cleaners by my wife and her lawyers, had lost my form, my sponsors and a lot of my so-called friends. I went looking for Jimmy who still haunted me after all these years but all I could find out was that he had hit the bottle and was homeless, somewhere in Scotland.

"When lightning starts, hold up your one iron and you'll be safe - even God can't hit a one iron" - Lee Trevino

I nearly lost my playing card one season after ten years on the tour, but somehow that provided the motivation and in the off season I went back to the South of Spain and played the same courses I had excelled on at the start of my professional career.

By this time I had divested myself of the entourage top professionals surround themselves with - coaches, gurus and shamans, I took the opportunity to test various golf clubs and balls from different manufacturers. Armed with a motley collection of clashing brands which individually felt good to me I set off with little fanfare to the first event of the New Year. Other newer kids on the block hogged the headlines by now and I enjoyed being under the radar and keeping out of the way of the media just as I imagine Jimmy would have done it.

Within a few events I was back to winning ways and soon was winning on both sides of the Atlantic, climbing the rankings and playing well in the top events. Finally 6 years ago I won a major, the Open - OK it was in England, not ideal for a Scotsman, but since there are only four a year and most top players only have a limited number of chances, I had the dreaded monkey off my back. I wasn't a journeyman but a proven winner able to compete all over the world at the highest level, and no one could take that away from me. I had been lucky with the weather that year and my unfashionable early start day on day one coupled with a late start day two captured the best conditions of both days. I could reel off the times I had played in Majors plodding through wind and rain and worn out greens in the early rounds with no chance of qualifying for the final two rounds let alone winning, despite playing well.

Whatever people said they couldn't take away from me the fact that I, Argent Brierley, was an Open winner and Major Champion. 'Argent' you may ask. Well, my parents liked this progressive rock band back in the 1970's before I was thought of. They had hits like 'God Gave Rock 'n' Roll to You', 'Liar' and 'I Don't Believe in Miracles' as well as the unhelpful, at least in the context of good golf swing, "Hold Your Head Up". Anyway, I had won 15 tournaments worldwide over the years so even although my best days were past I could still apparently make a living at corporate events. Mind you apart from cutting a tape, posing for a few photos, having lunch with the directors and perhaps giving them some golf tips I wasn't sure what else I could do. I began to wonder if I had done the right thing agreeing to attend. As often in those quiet moments, particularly as my flight wheeled over the Firth of Forth to make the dramatic approach to Edinburgh's Turnhouse Airport over Silverknowes, Bruntsfield and Royal Burgess golf courses, my thoughts turned to Jimmy Gibb.

30 Years Ago

Back in the day the Scottish Boys' Amateur Golf Championship was held at Dunbar links in East Lothian, about 20 miles down the River Forth from Edinburgh during the Easter holidays. I had played in it since I was 15 and this year was my last chance to win it before turning 18. I had come close in the last two years and recently was in good form, so was one of the favourites. Like the other competitors my Dad was with me and in those days we had a good relationship; he was a club professional and so golf was all around me from as long as I can remember. He never pushed me like Tiger Woods' Dad but subtly introduced me to the game, and when I became hooked, especially after an injury on the rugby field, I turned my back on team sports, focussed on golf and he did the rest.

Like the other boys I had all the kit, not just hand-me-downs, and was tricked out in my own bespoke clubs and matching clothing to suggest that I was a tour player for that manufacturer. How cool I thought I looked, but nowadays looking back on photos of these times I looked prematurely old, and not in the least a young rebel, more like Lena Zavaroni, the precocious young Scottish singer from back in the day who won talent contests singing songs from her parent's ancient record collection.

Dad and I travelled from Ayrshire, arriving a day or two beforehand and he caddied as I played the course a couple of times. We stayed at the Marine Hotel in nearby North Berwick, which was steeped in golf history and folklore.

I knew most of the top guys playing in the Boys' Championship and we chatted a bit in the locker room before the off and smiled at the new kids who arrived, all similarly decked out like adolescent tour pros with anxious parents in tow.

I will never forget the moment Jimmy

JIMMY GIBB (AGED 17)

Gibb arrived; the locker room door crashed open and it came this tall guy with an ancient worn leather pencil bag slung over his right shoulder, and a Tennant's lager plastic carrier bag in his other hand which seemed to contain a few bits and pieces. He had spiky hair, a scar down his left cheek and was wearing black drainpipes trousers, black suede brothel creeper shoes and a double breasted black cowboy-type shirt which had white piping on the front and cuffs. He didn't say anything and made to sit down at an empty part of the bench. "That's someone's seat!" I shouted. "Well he's no here," replied the newcomer. He took off his shoes revealing day-glo socks and proceeded to put on a plain pair of black golf shoes which had 'kilties,' fringed tongues covering the laces. That was a sartorial no-no which had gone out of fashion when Patty Berg retired from the US Women's Tour in the 1960's. "You're not wearing fucking kilties are you!" said one of my pals, Dave from

Aberdeen. "Looks like it, daddy's boy" he replied with a grim smile.

"Less of that, gentlemen!" said Major Smythe, one of the officials, drafted in from the Royal and Ancient Golf Club to oversee the competition. He turned to the newcomer "and who are you?" "Jimmy Gibb, I'm from the Fife Golfing Society" the newcomer replied in a broad accent. "Oh! -you're the one who isn't a member of a club". "Probably aye", he replied looking round the room at us and our golf wear with some disdain. "Well you're off in 10 minutes - you weren't here for the practice day?" "No I can just afford to come for the tournament days - it should be fun though" Jimmy replied deadpan. "Well you're too late for a locker," said the official. "I don't need one, this is all my stuff," he replied gesturing at the tatty golf bag, crumpled plastic bag and brothel creepers,

It was then I noticed his rag tag of clubs which rattled in the slim bag. His woods were still wooden, his irons thin blades which looked impossible to play and his putter, an ancient bronze Ping model which had developed a dark, blackish patina due to age and neglect.

This will be a laugh I thought. The format was match play knockout with 128 hopefuls playing best of 18 hole games until the remaining pair slugged out the final over 36 holes. My tie was not until midday and before I embarked on my hour long warm-up routine under the watchful eye of my father, I had time to watch this rough creature tee up at the first.

Jimmy walked out calmly despite the titters of those who pointed at his clothes, shoes and obsolete golf equipment. He did a few perfunctory swings exaggerating backswing and follow through, swivelled his shoulders a bit and stretched his back. He nonchalantly fished a ball out of the tiny pocket stitched to the side of his bag and then drew a 1 iron out of his bag, a club which all good golfers know is the most difficult, if not impossible club to play.

He calmly lost the toss and stood quietly beside his opponent's entourage while he drove off. It was a good shot down the fairway. "Do you not have a caddy?" asked his opponent as he picked up his golf tee. "No - you've just me to beat" said Jimmy without looking at him. He seemed already focussed on the shot. He dug his heel in the teeing ground and raised a bit of the turf, tamped it down a bit with the toe of his club and placed his ball on top - no tee for Jimmy! After a half- hearted looking practice swing he thrashed the ball down the fairway with a low penetrating trajectory and to my astonishment I saw the ball bound past his opponent's shot by about 20 yards. He pressed down the turf he had barely disturbed, then picked up his bag and swept off leaving his opponent and entourage in his wake.

By the time I had played a few holes of my tie Jimmy was walking back purposefully to the clubhouse with his opponent, the boy's father and the rest of that group walking miserably back. His erstwhile opponent was hitting the ground with his putter, repeatedly in frustration until the head of the blamed implement flew off. I heard later Jimmy won 9 holes up with 8 to play - his opponent had only managed to half one hole. The game had ended on a slightly sour note when he insisted his opponent hole out from 18 inches and the boy had missed. "That was so unfair and not within the spirit of golf" shouted the boy's father vicariously for his son whose temper had boiled over and had walked off the green without shaking hands. "Life can be pretty unfair too and I need to be back in Rosyth as soon as possible for my part-time job at the chip shop" replied Jimmy over his shoulder, without breaking stride.

Next day Jimmy turned up as before in what looked like the same clothes. I heard he caused some raised eyebrows when he bought 2 new golf balls from the pro shop rather than a box of a dozen or sleeve of 3 as we did. He didn't seem to lose many balls and it looked as though he wore them out.

He relentlessly cut through the next few rounds and was never taken beyond the 15th green. Suddenly I realised that if I made the final I was going to have to beat new boy, Jimmy. The only reverse Jimmy suffered in the run up to the final was when someone pissed into his brothel creepers while he was out on the course. Fortunately the smell of urine hit him before he put them on. He strode up and complained to Major Smythe who quickly retorted that it was not the organiser's fault. Jimmy said he did not think they would do such a childish thing but imagined they would wish to investigate his complaint which besmirched the good name of the host club and the R & A. No doubt he would require the shoes as evidence, or should he call on the Daily Record and give the evidence to them. With that he left the clubhouse, the spikes on his golf shoes clattering on the tarmac as he rushed off for the train.

When the day of the final arrived it was as I had predicted, me versus Jimmy.

Once again he turned up shortly before the tee-off time. It was a colder day and the only change in his attire was to wear black leather gloves on both hands and a 'C U Jimmy' novelty tartan hat with a pom-pom on top and strands of artificial red hair at the sides. "You can't wear that!" gasped Major Smythe pointing at the offending headgear. "Why not?" replied Jimmy. "There's nothing in the Rules of Golf about it and I am sure I saw in that picture of the Honourable Company of Edinburgh Golfers in Seventeen Something they're wearing bunnets like this, besides I am celebrating getting to the final." The hat stayed, and I must admit it did distract me a bit although I tried not to show it.

I soon realised that he was a doughty opponent who put me under pressure but seemed to be playing within himself. I was one of the longer hitters in the tournament, but most of the time he contented himself hitting low raking iron shots off the tee which landed behind my ball then, playing first, he invariably put the ball on the green challenging me to try and equal or better his shot.

The match was close and I kept in touch thanks to the odd bad bounce Jimmy suffered and a few of his putts which just failed to drop despite his deft touch on the greens. We were all square after 18 holes and took lunch, which was just as well. A heavy front of rain passed over and lashed the course for 30 minutes then it eased off but still kept drizzling. When we came out for the second round I noticed Jimmy had a yellow cagoule doubled over the strap of his bag. As the match progressed and the rain became heavier he eventually put this garment on. By this time his tartan hat was looking a bit soggy and when he holed a longish putt at the 4th to go 1 up he threw it into the crowd. The rain increased and Jimmy just pulled the hood up of his thin nylon anorak. He pulled his hood back for tee shots and most putts but kept it up for the rest! Needless to say he eschewed all offers of an umbrella saying that he preferred keeping his hands in his pockets between shots.

I did feel that the hood and Jimmy's stubbornness was working in my favour; my Dad confirmed as much when we had a confab between shots - "you've got him, son".

But it didn't work that way and suddenly over the last 5 holes it seemed Jimmy changed gear and birdied 4 holes in a row to win 3 up with 2 to go. I had taken him past the 15th green - but not by much. I was stunned but I felt I was in the presence of a great talent. My Dad was angry and started scrutinising Jimmy's clubs to see if any were illegal or he had a 15th club in the bag by mistake. "Well played, that was a great game!" I said. "Do you fancy a quick drink before we go?" "I'll need to catch the next train" he replied. "Don't worry, I am sure my Dad will give you a lift back - it's on our way"

So our friendship was formed. Jimmy told me he had been left abandoned in a shoe box on a doorstep in Grangemouth as a baby and grew up in children's homes until he was fostered out with an old couple and learned to play golf from his foster father. Once he told me he felt an affinity with Superman who had also been found as a baby on a doorstep having been sent in a rocket by his parents as their planet Krypton was failing!

Present Day

I woke with a jolt as the landing gear of the plane was extended for the final approach. Shortly afterwards I reached the concourse and travelling light, with just a carry-on bag and no golf clubs I soon reached the taxi rank. "The Balmoral Hotel, Princes Street, please." I said to an ancient cabbie. "Aye, no problem son, I ken the way, there's only one Bal-mor-al" he said exaggerating the components' of the name.

"Do I no ken you fae somewhere, Bud?" said the cabbie eying me in his mirror. "Probably a Wanted poster!" I retorted irritated at his lack of recognition of me in my home country. A few miles later he said "I ken now, you used to be a golfer!" "I still am, it's just the courses that got longer" I replied, pleased with myself at parodying a line from the old black and white classic "Sunset Boulevard". The cabbie deadpanned me again. "Did ye no win some tournament?" "Aye a few, no big deal." I remarked closing down the conversation before my ego was further dented. "There's no way that old bastard's getting a tip!", I thought to myself.

However I enjoyed the trip down memory lane as we headed into the city centre and I caught sight of Edinburgh Castle perched high on a rock with the unusual form of Arthur's Seat, more volcanic debris in the background.

The cabbie swiftly got out of his seat when we reached the hotel and opened the door for me. "You're that Argent boy. A'm sorry a could'nae place you right away without a club in your hands." "Yes pity I didn't have one," I smiled grimly and thrust the fare and a £10 note into his wrinkled hand.

I was made most welcome by the staff at my hotel reception and offered a complementary dram of whisky which I managed to down and set off for my room on the 3rd floor eschewing all efforts to carry my small bag.

I had been put up in a suite at the New Balmoral Hotel above Waverley Station a short distance from Jenners. I was a day early deliberately and had arranged to speak to their PR people about final arrangements for the opening. A light lunch had been arranged in their offices and as the lift door opened at my destination my way was blocked by a tall man wearing Jenners overalls. I was so pre-occupied I didn't look at him properly and tried to edge past when an unmistakeable voice rang out "Do ye no' recognise your old pal, Argie?"

The years had not been particularly kind but the eyes were never to be forgotten. "Jimmy!" I shouted and instinctively dropped my bag and grabbed him in a big hug. "There's hardly a day I don't think of you and wondered what happened." "Aye well, you went on the golf tour and I hit the bevvy and went a tour of homeless hostels for a few years. Actually in the summer I preferred living in a tent up Corstorphine Hill, listening to the wild animals from the zoo and watching wild swingers hacking their way round Murrayfield Golf Course. One day I saw a boy I played in that Championship we played together in at Dunbar - the one I beat silly in the first round. I recognised his swing - a bit old fashioned these days - his Dad must have taught him. When he was on his own one day I went down and introduced myself. He seemed to have heard all about my troubles and apologised for not shaking my hand all these years back. He asked if I was interested in a job as night porter here and I've never looked back once I got sorted out. I have my own flat on the premises and as you know I quite liked being up late at night and early in the morning. I saw you were coming to do the opening and I wondered what you were like these days."

"Do you play any golf?" I asked without thinking. "No" he laughed. I've seen photos of these guys doing a full swing on one leg but most of the time you end up on your arse." My wooden leg is old-school compared to the new stuff out now but I'm happy sometimes when I have a quiet spell in the afternoons to go across the road and play on the putting green. I still have that old Ping putter. I buried it when I was desperate so that I wouldn't sell it for drink". "I'm here until tomorrow night - how about a challenge match tomorrow afternoon - pound a hole as in the good old days?" "You're on," Jimmy replied, and shook my hand with his famous vice-like grip. "It'll be like James Bond versus Oddjob". "Actually Bond played Goldfinger and Oddjob tried to even things up" I replied.

I went into the meeting to find some rather glum-faced PR people. Apparently an ageing golf star was not as big a draw as they had thought and I could sense in the room a feeling that perhaps the generous appearance fee they had offered was now considered to have been a bit rash.

"We feel we need a bit of an angle for the press release ahead of the opening tomorrow. I don't suppose you have any ideas?" said Brodie, the leader of the PR delegation - a smooth looking man in his forties in an expensive suit, white shirt and no tie - a clothing combo which I particularly detested especially as it had come into vogue when David Cameron was our Prime Minister. "Well as you know I'm not much good at these things and have been flattered to have received your kind invitation. I'm not about to sign a major sponsorship deal and am not dating anyone famous - well no one at all at the moment" I said winking at his attractive assistant Nicole," but I might have just the thing for you, if you can make some snappy copy".

I told them my tale and of the great match scheduled for tomorrow. "Brilliant" said one of the directors and I realised he must be the losing golfer from the Boys' Championship that Jimmy had mentioned. "I didn't realise you two went so far back."

"So tomorrow we have the opening ceremony and reception, then cross the road to Princes Street Gardens to play putting?" said Brodie. "Yes I replied; all you need to do is get the Council to cut the grass short for the occasion so it is like a proper golf green, and get me a Scotty Cameron Newport 2 putter like the one Tiger Woods uses and a few Titleist Pro VI x balls."

I just had time that night to have a few practice putts on my hotel bedroom carpet. I had to spend most of it with the PR people and put a speech together for the grand opening.

A good sized crowd watches the 'Open Champion v Boys' Champion – rematch' on the putting green in East Princess Street Gardens

I was very nervous next morning in what was a straightforward occasion with a good-sized but not huge crowd. I managed to deliver my speech, answer questions, pose for photos and numerous selfies and sign countless autographs.

I did manage time for a sandwich and a cup of tea then walked across the road to Princes Street Gardens where Jimmy was waiting for me with his customary calm smile. He was still wearing his Jenner's overalls and instantly I could see that he still had his trusty putter which proudly displayed 50 years' of abuse and use. There were lots more cameras and film crews; I was amazed at the interest but the PR duo had whipped up a storm with copy like 'Open Champion v Boys' Champion – rematch'. Furthermore, this modest little municipal putting green was set against the stunning backcloth of Jenner's Stores, the Sir Walter Scott Monument and towering above all else, Edinburgh Castle,

I could see that Jimmy was up for it but it was not difficult for me to muster my competitive instincts which had been honed over the years on the professional tours.

I smiled inwardly when I saw Jimmy was slightly disconcerted by the closely mown grass and I managed to win 2 of the first 3 holes and kept this lead up to the 9th hole. I could see however that Jimmy had lost none of his putting skill and once he adjusted to the faster surface he left most of his putts close for twos. Finally at the 10th hole he sunk a long putt for a hole-in-one and although I went close my ball didn't follow his in. A few holes on he was level and then over the remaining few holes his game was peerless and he won most of them to edge ahead. I had been hoping to win the last hole to half the match but Jimmy, whose first shot had not been his best holed a longish right to left curler.

I couldn't beat that and instinctively ran over to Jimmy, shook his hand and raised it aloft. "You jammy bugger!" I said with a grin. "I can still beat you" Jimmy replied. "You know", he continued, "I've come to terms with things over the years. I was pleased for you, when you won the Open and all these tournaments but reckoned I could have done better".

We couldn't have done better - the picture of me holding Jimmy's hand up went viral and I did lots of interviews about the match and our past. I lost a game but regained a friend and had that photograph to put on my mantelpiece with the one of the motley crew form the Boys' Championship - all of us kids trying to look like pros except Jimmy standing there in his logo-less post-punk gear staring at the camera with nonchalant smile.

The Thirties' Man

Chapter 1 – The Duke

Of all the characters who were members of Silverfield Golf Club during my time there, the 'Thirties Man' must rank as one of the most bizarre.

The nickname - never used to his face however, neatly summarized his mode of dress, golf gear, mode of transport and, as I was to find out, way of life. At times I struggled to remember his name, Ruaridh Morrison, because we all called him 'The Duke' as he bore a startling resemblance to the Duke of Windsor circa 1937.

When I joined the club more than 30 years ago the Duke was by far the most striking member and as he was a regular at the course I soon bumped into him and played alongside him at monthly medals.

"Give me golf clubs, fresh air and a beautiful partner, and you can keep the clubs and the fresh air." - Jack Benny

You always knew he was there as he arrived in a beautiful 1930's supercharged sports car called a 'Squire' which was maroon with black wings and very rakish - no windscreen just a couple of aero screens. It had a raucous engine and the Duke could be seen in the car park on many occasions tuning the twin SU carburettors to control a misfire which often resulted in flames coming out of the exhaust during gear changes.

When the car was in good order it would be driven in through the gates with a flourish and parked at the same spot beside some bushes whereupon the Duke jumped over the low door rather than open it, and inevitably was resplendent in plus 4's, tweed jacket, check shirt, cravat and brown brogues, topped with a smart bunnet of the type sported by trainers of National Hunt racehorses.

The car was open topped and had no hood but a tonneau cover was drawn over the passenger side from which would be produced the legendary olive coloured canvas bag with leather trim which contained a vintage set of clubs.

The Duke did have hickory clubs and used them to good effect each year in the Hickory Golf Open where he finished 4th one year. No mean feat as one year Sandy Lyle, a past winner of the Open and the Masters triumphed. For club purposes, the Duke used a set of E R Whitcombe irons from the 1930s which boasted steel shafts but were finished to look like wooden shafts. They were beautiful irons produced by the elder brother of the 1938 winner of The Open, Reg Whitcombe. They were bladed irons but had a V shaped back to concentrate the power of the club within a narrow but specific sweet spot. The woods had similar shafts and genuine wooden heads with brass soles which pronounced there purpose as well as their number 1 'The Driver', 2 'The Brassie' and number 3 'The Spoon. They were a matched set made by George Nicoll of Leven and bore the legendary name of Henry Cotton on their heads - he was the winner of the Open in 1934, 1937 and 1948.

As for the putter, this was an ancient hickory shafted number which back in the day would have been called a cleek, a simple blade forged by Joe Anderson of Perth according to the inscription. This was kept oily to prevent it rusting too much. It had a lot of loft for a putter which meant when the Duke hit the ball it skipped for the first few inches before rolling towards the flag. It looked awkward on modern fat closely cut greens but the Duke was a master with it from off the green and light rough as the ball just seemed to float out of the grass and roll up close to or into the hole.

I was quietly in awe of the man as he quietly exuded cool, like Thin White Duke period David Bowie. For all I know perhaps Bowie spotted the Duke on one of his many trips up to Edinburgh, and filed away the look for future exploitation.

I was quietly curious too and was amazed and impressed when I checked the roll of members that his handicap was 6.4 which was way better than me, replete with modern kit and struggling off 13.7!

Chapter 2 – Foursomes

After a year or two at the club during which time I had developed a nodding acquaintance with the Duke I first experienced his art at close quarters when I was drawn against him and his partner Big Roy in the Mens' foursomes competition.

Foursomes was not my favourite mode of play It is part and parcel of the membership at Muirfield but I found I could never get warmed up playing half the normal shots in a round and often from unusual angles and locations on the course as my luck was to play with a hooker whose shots ended up on the left hand rough, compared to the right hand rough familiar to me after one of my slices.

This competition was taken seriously by most of the male members of the club and most entries comprised longstanding partnerships, whereas I, as a new member, simply entered and asked to be assigned a partner who was usually elderly, bespectacled and an erratic high handicapper. As soon as I met my partner for the first time on the first tee of the first round I realised we were unlikely to progress much further and the final indignity was walking in from a far flung part of the course after a heavy defeat on the 11th green.

This year was slightly different and my new partner was Bob Munroe, the no nonsense head of a plumbing company who had worked his way up in the trade from leaving school at 15, to managing a well-respected local company he had founded 20 years previously. He was now able to take a more hands off role far from the choked drains and broken toilets which had been his stock in trade to overseeing his workmen on large contracts for building firms, and spending plenty of time honing his love of the game of golf. He lacked my experience and subtlety but had big strong hands and wrists and had little difficulty putting the partnership back on the straight and narrow when my tee shots landed him in thick rough.

We hit it off as a team passed the time with chat between shots and won our first match comfortably.

When I wrote our names on the notice board as winners of the tie I noticed our opponents' names were already in place - Roy Gibson & Ruaridh Morrison, past champions of the competition and perennial contenders for a place in the final rounds.

I volunteered to phone the Duke, again out of curiosity to see if the call was answered by a butler or a maid but the call was taken by the man himself in his now familiar clipped tones. "So you saw off these old boys, young man" said the Duke. "Yes sir" I replied out of deference and an awkwardness not knowing what to call him. "None of that stuff, young man-just call me Ruaridh - everybody else does!" he

THE DUKE (RUARIDH MORRISON)

said with an infectious laugh well knowing the untruth of that statement.

We settled on the following Tuesday evening at 5 30 for our tie and I spent the time in between filled with excitement and anticipation of the match.

It was a fine evening and there would be plenty of time to play a full round if need be and perhaps even play up the first again if still tied. Alas that was not to be and we were soon on the back foot due to Roy's booming drives and the Duke's accuracy and consistency. His shots never placed his partner in any trouble and usually gave him the optimum position for the next shot. He was able to shape the ball one way or the other cutting off corners, bending round trees and bunkers and putted extremely well.

He was a joy to watch with his languid old fashioned swing starting with a forward press of his club before the backswing, a pause at the top and a rapidly accelerating downswing and stylish but effortless follow through.

Of course I shouldn't have been watching him so closely and just concentrating on my own game. We rallied a bit around the turn when Big Roy lost their ball at one hole and again when he missed a short downhill putt my partner refused to concede. "he's rubbish at these ones" whispered my partner - and he was right. Roy had putted boldly down the slope taking the break out of the putt but instead the ball went scuttling 10 feet past and for once the Duke was unable to hole the return.

Our rally was too little too late and we shook hands on the 15th green having gone 4 down with only 3 left to play.

We had a convivial drink afterwards and I was given a guided tour of the Squire sports car after I had asked about it and used some pre-existing knowledge of the vehicle gleaned from a book on British vintage cars my Dad gave me one Christmas when I was a boy.

Towards the end of the year we heard the sad news that Big Roy was stricken with cancer. At first news was conflicting but he had an emergency operation and was to be given a course of radiotherapy and the next we heard he had allowed his membership to lapse.

Chapter 3 – New Foursomes partner

It was customary to apply to play in the match play competitions early in the year but for some reason, probably being busy at work I omitted to do so. I did stick my name down to play in the first monthly medal of the year customarily held at the end of February.

When I turned up for the 8:54 tee time I was surprised to see The Duke had put his name down for this slot also and he greeted me warmly like an old friend. It all became clear when at the tricky 5th he surprisingly put his ball into the same piece of thick rough that I had already landed in. We poked away for a few minutes looking for the elusive spheres when the Duke suddenly said "I don't suppose you would partner me in the Mens' foursomes this year, Jock? The prognosis for poor Roy doesn't sound good. I think you and I could cheer him up by doing well in the competition."

I was taken aback but regained my composure when I found my ball in a difficult lie at the foot of a tuft of grass. "But I'm not in Big Roy's league!" I replied. "Maybe not but you hit a decent ball and I think we could play well together aided by your handicap." "I'd be delighted" I gushed. I was elated and this feeling of euphoria carried me through the round and my handicap came down to 13.4 as a result.

I put in my application along with the Duke's and couldn't wait until the draw took place at the end of March.

Our first round match went well as our elderly opponents, despite mustering combined handicaps of 50, fell away in the rain when their thick glasses began to mist up and yips started to form part of their putting strokes. The Duke and I had a leisurely drink afterwards as our opponents hurried off home to their spouses but when teased about being under the thumb by the Duke they blamed their waterworks as they lived at the other side of Edinburgh!

And so that summer every 3 or 4 weeks we had another tie and progressed to the next round. Under the Duke's subtle captaincy I was playing better and once he had determined that the optimum formation for us was for me to drive off at the first hole - a role previously carried out by Big Roy, we prevailed in a couple of close matches one of which involved me teeing off at the 19th after we had finished all square.

I began to believe we could win the tournament even when it became apparent we were up against the demon combination in the final of 'Lanky' Strachan, a tall former athlete and winner of the Powderhall Sprint for professional runners. He was new to golf, had a high handicap in the 20s which he protected but being a fit man having spent a lot of time working out with a medicine ball, he could hit a very long drive albeit his accuracy left something to be desired. He was paired with Tony Roberts whom I called 'Bouffant Boy' on account of his improbably golden back-combed and quiffed locks. He was a former club champion and although in his early 50s was still playing off 3 and was a very competitive man.

After a poor drive by me off the first tee we were soon one down and immediately lost the second after I failed to convert a birdie chance following a deft approach shot to the green by the Duke. Bouffant Boy had a rigid putting style but was deadly from about 8 feet in.

However Duke and I stopped the rot and after halving holes into the second nine we won one back at the short 13th after a great tee shot by my partner and me converting the remaining tiddler. We won the 17th after I hit my best drive and our partners ended up lost in the bushes. The 18th is an awkward hole - challenging but with so many slopes is often settled by one side hitting a bad shot leaving the result in no doubt before the green is reached. This time we were fairly evenly matched going down the long fairway. We were shorter and more accurate and were hitting our next shot from good spots which proved as effective as our opponents' length was blunted by having to hack out of rough, or playing off a slope with the ball above the feet requiring the club to be gripped lower on the shaft, which reduced the length of shot possible from that position.

We were 20 feet from the flag with our opposition closer but in a bunker. Duke lined up the putt with his elderly implement but for once duffed the shot and the ball only rolled about 10 feet. However Lanky's bunker shot hit the lip of the trap, the ball ricocheted vertically up in the air and fell back into the sand albeit in an easier position.

Bouffant Boy who had been on the green waiting with his putter grimly walked off to his bag where he selected his sand wedge and left his putter resting by the bag. You could see he was bristling but he seemed to thrive on pressure and produced an excellent shot with the ball landing softly on the green and rolling up to the edge of the hole. The ball refused to drop but we readily conceded the remaining putt leaving me with a testy 10 footer which was slightly downhill and bent to the left. Duke left it all to me and I took my time hitting the ball confidently to ensure it reached the hole as it wouldn't matter if it sailed miles past. The ball seemed to do a full lap of the rim of the cup before falling in!

Chapter 4 – My new best friend

We were Foursomes club champions! Duke was very generous in his praise in contrast to our opponents who were polite but clearly quietly beating themselves up for being beaten by a poseur with 60 year old clubs and a middle handicap golfer with a dodgy swing.

That win cemented my friendship with the Duke, and although we never won the Foursomes again we went close several times and were recognised as doughty opponents. Duke and I always partnered each other in medals and often in bounce games over the ensuing 15 years. We sat beside each other at golf dinners too but apart from that I knew little more about the Duke and never was invited to or visited his house. I had never thought to consider how old he was as he seemed timeless but one day, when we were due to play in the Autumn Medal I began to get a bit anxious that Duke was going to be late for our 9:12 tee time. About 9:05 I heard the familiar thrum of the Squire and then its engine backfired as the Duke slowed to turn into the clubhouse car park. He did his usual sweeping turn into his parking spot, killed the engine then did his usual jump over the drivers' door only this time his right leg caught the top of the door and he fell heavily on the tarmac. I rushed over to him and was quickly joined by other golfers who were unloading their cars in preparation for their later matches.

"I'll be OK said the Duke - I'm just a silly old bugger who was late and in too much of a hurry," He had a badly cut knee and a bump on his head. It was agreed the others would tee off early and we were given a free time later in the morning. Duke and I went for a coffee after he had some First Aid - he refused to go for a check-up.

"Maybe I 'm getting to old for all this caper" said the Duke. "I haven't been feeling so good recently." "Perhaps you should see your doctor next week for a health check" I said hypocritically, as it was something I would never do myself. A few minutes later Duke started shaking, fell on the floor and had some sort of fit. I shouted to the bar staff who were still setting up for opening time beloved by early starters and those older members whose golfing faculties had diminished to an extent that they no longer wielded any clubs. They did however retain membership on a reduced basis to continue to enjoy the subsidised drinks prices. Someone dialled 999 and when an ambulance came I did the talking and ended up going off to hospital with the Duke performing the sort of next-of-kin/witness role.

During the journey the Duke lost consciousness and the trip to the hospital became a blue light job. I was kept back as the Duke was taken into Accident & Emergency. I waited for hours with only a two year old tatty golf magazine for company in the waiting room. It was full of adverts for then new clubs which were now well out of date, declaimed as rubbish in favour of newer more shiny equipment with even more complex claims about the basis why extra length and accuracy could be secured at a premium price.

Chapter 5 – The Endgame

I fell asleep but then was gently woken by a doctor and nurse. Although drowsy I soon twigged from their expressions it was serious. "I am afraid your friend Mr Morrison has died. He had a sudden brain haemorrhage" said the young doctor. "I have a feeling an aneurysm had been developing and the fall may have exacerbated it". I was shocked at the suddenness of the news. "Did he ever regain consciousness?" I asked, thinking of nothing better to say. "Oh yes he did," said the nurse who I noticed had a badge with 'Sandra' on it. "He was conscious for a few minutes before the final incident. He apologized for you missing your game today but asked me to thank you for being his friend and putting up with his eccentricities."

I was told the Duke had left details in his wallet that I was his next-of-kin and Mr MacRoberts of Breakspears Solicitors his executors. I agreed to telephone the solicitors first thing on Monday. I found out however that Mr MacRoberts had died some years ago and was put through to Ms Lascelles who had never met the Duke but undertook to check the file. I told her about the duke's car still languishing in the club car park and she arranged to have it brought to the Duke's home which had a garage where the car was normally stored.

I was shocked when I attended at the solicitor's office a fortnight later and met the smart and efficient Ms Lascelles to be told that the Duke had left his entire estate, house, car, possessions and shares to me. "Why me?" I asked. "Well he had no relatives. His mother died when he was an infant and neither she nor his father seemed to have any surviving relatives - Mr Morrison was 75 you know." "I didn't actually; he seemed to look about 50 all the years I've known him." "Well he lived a very austere life like he was in the 1930s." said Ms Lascelles. "He golfed like that too!" I exclaimed. "I suggest I let you see the house you've inherited". Shortly afterwards I was driven in Ms Lascelles new Mazda MX 5 sports car to the bungalow in Blackhall which had been the Duke homestead. It was a neat detached house with a 1930s Art Deco pagoda-style roof, a detached garage and a large garden due to it being tucked into the end of a cul de sac.

The front garden was still fairly neat despite the lawn needing to be mown. In the back garden were substantial vegetable areas, a mini orchard of trees and gooseberry and blackcurrant bushes and a line of raspberry canes. All in all the Duke had been industrious when not out on the links and it looked as though he had enough growing to be self-sufficient.

In the garage lay the Squire under a dust sheet. I pulled it off and admired the gleaming body and the leather seats with just the right patina of age. "What a beautiful old girl!", I gasped, unaware of Ms Lascelles' grimace at the impractical vehicle and my politically incorrect analogy.

The inside of the house was a revelation. It was like stepping into a pre-war museum piece. It was old but like the Squire well maintained and tidy. There was an imposing T-shaped hall covered in panelling but a roof light from the attic space provided sufficient illumination during the day to prevent it from being gloomy. There was an ancient looking but clean and serviceable gas cooker on stilt-like legs, a large double porcelain Belfast sink, a wringer, a clothes pulley and a larder, but no fridge. The Duke certainly lived the life. In the lounge were comfortable chintz chairs and a sofa. There was a 78 gramophone and 'Sunray' radio but no television.

"It's timeless!" I gushed. Ms Lascelles seemed to shudder, she was a modern girl and I could see it was not her idea of a home. I was captivated. "We can market it for you if you wish." she said. "No I think I'd like to keep it. I have a fairly modern boring flat in Haymarket. Could you sell that for me instead?" She shrugged. Another weird client she thought but it was business.

Chapter 6 – Epilogue

So it came about the following year, when the season opened, properly to my mind with the first of the club singles ties to be played in early April, I roared into the car park in the Squire, screeched to a halt and jumped over the driver's door revealing my new tweeds and plus fours and rakish bunnet. I walked round the car, rummaged under the tonneau and pulled out the tatty bag of 70 year-old clubs and strode towards the starter's hut.

I had become the 30s' man.

The Deal

Chapter 1 – Jock's half-day skive

I had skived off work, and felt like a guilty second year schoolboy skipping lessons I hated, swapping them for the fresh air.

Actually in July work is often in the doldrums, and with many people at the office on holiday your time was either spent sorting out mess they had left behind or the phone remained silent and the daily hordes of e mails reduced mostly to spam which were quickly deleted *en masse*.

I had planned this Wednesday golf game for some while and anxiously checked the forecast hoping it would be a decent day. The truth was I would have played in any weather until the elements made it impossible, or more likely the club manager stopped play.

I contrived to have a meeting out of the office late morning and let it be known the other attendees were great bores and I probably would not make it back. My old MGB GT was in the car park with the clubs stowed under some cardboard boxes and I would pick a trolley up at the club since it was going to be a hot day. I had a new 20 degree rescue club in my bag that I was anxious to try out, and armed with a sandwich, a fruity drink and a sleeve of 3 new balls what could possibly go wrong?

The course was deserted and Johnny, the pro, reckoned not many people would be out until the hordes started arriving from work about 4 30 for an evening tie. "Lucky

I have a half day today and everything has turned out fine," I lied and set off.

Despite these guilty feelings I hit a decent tee shot at the first and just missed out on a par at what can be a testing start. I trundled on scoring in line with my 12 handicap and was pleased at the 5th to hit a fine shot over the blind approach to the green with my new club. Sure enough I was on the green and two putts later I had a satisfactory par.

It was only then, as I walked down to the 6th tee that I was surprised to see players ahead of me. Normally as you played up and down the first few holes you would be aware of who was a few holes ahead, and who you might catch up in the second nine. They were 200 yards or so down the fairway and had just played their second shots, neither of which had troubled the green at this short, but tight par 4. I could only assume Big Dan Foulkes and The Hon. John McDermid had been looking for a rather long time for their balls in the trees or gorse which took up most of the left-hand rough.

Dan and John were characters in their own way and I was surprised to see these business rivals playing golf together. Dan was of Irish working class stock but had built up a successful building company, starting out as a joiner with a wheelbarrow for his tools. On the other hand the Hon. John was posh, son and now heir to Sir Peregrine McDermid who himself had inherited an large engineering company which has prospered during the Second World War and ever since, subtly altering its focus from shipbuilding to North Sea Oil and more recently bridge building and motorway contracts.

"I know I am getting better at golf because I am hitting fewer spectators." - Gerald R. Ford

As the two men joined each other from opposite sides of the fairway and walked towards the hole they stopped, chatted for a few minutes then shook hands. What seemed odd at the time was that they then laboriously 3- putted out on the green then set off for the next tee which was out of sight over a small rise.

I don't think they saw me, as they appeared so engrossed. I sat down and rewarded myself with a drink and half of my sandwich. There was a light breeze and some of the contents of the tee box had blown out or perhaps the seagulls had been scavenging about. I picked up the bits and pieces and then noticed a piece of folded A4 paper with _HEADS OF AGREEMENT_ at the top. I wondered if it was important and had been dropped by the duo ahead of me. I thought the better of reading it and stuffed it in my bag. As it happens I have a big golf bag a proper Tour professional's once used by Argent Brierley at the start of his career before he had a lucky week and won the Open a few years ago. He was a bit of a journeyman and had his ups and downs after a few tournament wins at the start of his playing days until it all got to his head. His wife chucked him out and took all his golf stuff to the Shelter shop in Stockbridge. Being a posh suburb of Edinburgh it is amazing the things toffs throw out and one wet day as I was walking along Raeburn Place in Stockbridge I saw his old bag in the window for £10!

By the time I had played the 6th in a straightforward manner with a drive and a wedge to the green and almost a birdie, then ascended to the 7th tee Dan and Hon. John had disappeared. They had obviously made short work of that par 3 and walked up the 8th tee out of my view.

Although they were pretty poor players and had handicaps in the mid-20s, it did not stop either of them being as competitive on the course as they obviously were in business. Dan had Honma golf clubs and matching apparel. Honma is an up-market Japanese brand which has had a good record of making fine clubs used by top pros but nowadays taps the super-rich market, and Dan's woods and irons with gold inserts were said to have cost £4,000 a club. Fortunately the soles of the club were made of more robust metals as Dan duffed his way around Silverfield not realising that physical strength, gained on the building site, was not a prerequisite for a good golf swing.

The Hon. John had inherited most of his clubs like everything else. They were a fine set of Wilson Staff irons of the type used by Nick Faldo back in the 1990s. He even had a Wilson TPA XVIII flange bladed putter of the type which Faldo used to win back-to-back Masters. Hon. John seemed reasonably proficient with this club which was just as well as he often took ages and many strokes to reach the green.

I once played him in a tie which finished on the 14th green when I drubbed him 6 & 4. I indicated that I admired the putter which you rarely saw nowadays, save in the form of expensive copies made by other companies. Anyway the Hon. John made it clear he was not getting rid of it and would see him out. "You have to stick by the most important club in the bag and realise that if it is not working then you are not working." Sage words but notwithstanding I keep looking in charity shops and second hand racks for one to this day!

I had also played against Big Dan who had a bit of a reputation as a cheat but like most competitive but hopeless golfers he moaned about really bad shots of which he had a few per round - fresh air ones, shanks and complete duffs which moved the ball a few feet. In the interests of having a more competitive game

I offered mulligans which were readily and unashamedly accepted after which usually a decent shot was played. He was quite good fun to play with a fund of stories about working on building sites, the best one being when two navvies fell out on the job about bricklaying and had a square go with each other using JCB diggers! Fortunately neither was injured but the machines were badly damaged and the disputed wall reduced to rubble. They were otherwise good workers and Dan fined them but allowed them to keep working provided they didn't touch the machinery.

I next caught a glimpse of Big Dan and the Hon. John as they tacked their way up the 11th fairway. I had been delayed looking for a ball and was just taking my time since I had no standing on the course according to the rules and etiquette of golf and I knew, since they were deeply engrossed in their game, they would be unlikely to wave me through.

Gradually however I caught up with them thanks to some solid rescue shots when I had driven into the rough or just needed a solid shot between 150 and 180 yards to the green. I still kept my distance but Big Dan and The Hon. John were slowing appreciably as often happens when a match reaches the *denouement*.

I held back to let them finish the 16th and expressed disinterest other than to offer a cheery wave as they walked to the next tee so as to reassure them I was not pressing them but they did not acknowledge me. I made quick work of the 16th thanks to a lucky long putt from the front edge having under-clubbed my approach. Overall I was quite pleased with my game and in good shape for the Monthly Medal that weekend. I resolved to put my name down for a tee-off time when I got back to the Club House. With my new rescue club I felt I could score well and perhaps improve my handicap a notch, if not winning a prize.

I was in pole position to watch them play out the 17th. Both men had hit reasonable drives which ended up on the fairway albeit on opposite sides. There was some chat between them about who was to play first - none of this whoever is ready first plays rather the old rule who was further away had to play first and show his hand. In the event both men were short of the green by a few yards even although they only had to play a decent 8 iron shot. They had swapped sides by then and Dan was now on the right of the green having narrowly missed a bunker. He had to play first and sensibly, for a duffer, putted and ended up about 6 feet from the pin. The Hon. John elected to chip his shot but duffed it and left it 15 feet short-game on!

John missed his next putt and indeed the ball soared past the hole - he obviously had gone for the hole and now had and 8-10 foot putt to finish. He missed that too, but still would not concede, although fortunately Big Dan ended this indifferent passage of play by holing his putt for a par 4 albeit the ball bobbled round the cup for a bit before falling in.

John offered his hand and they doffed their hats to each other - Dan's bunnet and the Hon. John's Panama with a green and gold silk band. They packed up their kit and didn't bother walking back to the 18th tee or indeed dropping balls down the fairway beside the cart path back to the 17th.

By the time I played the 17th and to my annoyance, scored a 5 which I blamed on having watched the poor stroke play of my predecessors, Big Dan and the Hon. John had walked down the whole of the 18th, by-passed the green and gone into the clubhouse.

Chapter 2 – Guilty Conscience

I would have joined them for a cool drink but I guiltily thought I'd better check my mobile phone which had been on silent in my bag. I was horrified to find 10 missed calls and 6 phone messages, most from the office. I played the last one and heard an exasperated Sybil from the office in tears saying "please get in touch quickly. Your Dad has had a stroke and has been rushed off to the Edinburgh Royal Infirmary. By the way where the hell have you been; I hope you haven't been golfing?"

By the time I got to the hospital Dad was in theatre and Mum and her sister Auntie Ruby were sitting in the corridor tearful. "Where the hell have you been, Jock? You're Mum's past herself." "I was out of the office at a meeting." I replied as blandly as I could. "You look like you've been golfing." "Well I had a few holes practice on the way back." I explained realising my casual attire and sunburnt face were incompatible with a day spent in office surroundings. "Humph!" was Ruby's only response. As ever it was what was not said that spoke volumes as she dismissed my weak pathetic and largely untrue position.

Eventually Mum spoke. Dad had been pottering in the garden and although Mum had asked him to come in he insisted on finishing off tending his beloved begonias. She heard him fall and found him unconscious on the path twitching slightly.

All they had found out was he had had a stroke which had affected his left side and unable to speak but it was early days. After scans they had decided to operate on the blood clot and were hopeful although the next 48 hours would be crucial.

Dad did pull through but his speech was difficult to follow, except for Mum and I and he walked slowly with a crutch. He was returned home after a couple of weeks and Mum and I, with odd bits or nursing help, had a busy time over the next 12 months. His beloved begonias died in the ground. I knew they had to be lifted and put in the potting shed in sand at the end of the season but there was little time to think of such things.

That included golf. Needless to say I didn't make the July medal and didn't play for the rest of the year.

Things were so bad at home helping out that I even toyed with not renewing my subscription, but I knew how happy Dad was a few years back when I had stopped feeling sorry for myself having been dumped by a girlfriend, cut the drink and got back to playing some serious golf.

Chapter 3 – Back home

Although I had my own flat I ended up staying back at home in the room I had last used as a teenager. There were still Airfix model Spitfires, Hurricanes and Mosquito aircraft on threads hanging from the ceiling swaying slightly in the breeze but to my mind were in a dog fight with the Messerschmitt Bf 109s, Focke-Wulf Fw 190s and Heinkel He 111s dangling at the other side of the room.

I couldn't be bothered changing the décor as busy days at the office were flanked by early mornings helping get Dad up, showered and dressed and then putting him to bed at night. Mum bore the brunt and after a few months looked totally knackered so I sent her off to Majorca for a week with her sister Ruby and with extra help from community nurses gave her a bit of a break. Dad didn't want to see his friends as he felt frustrated by not being able to speak clearly and be understood. Mum and I by comparison had tuned into his new mode of speech and understood most of what he said and glossed around the difficult bits to avoid frustrating him.

One day when Mum and I were having a cup of tea and Dad had gone into one of his deep mid-afternoon sleeps from which he often woke up temporarily disorientated, she suggested I go and have a game of golf. "You haven't played in ages and you mustn't feel guilty about that game you were having the day Dad had his stroke."

"Why don't you go and play in one of these medals you used to talk about. I'll get Ruby to come over and help." "I don't think she will be party to me skiving off for a game of golf" I replied. "Not at all," replied Mum, "it was her idea as she thought you had worked awfully hard this past year and you know we really enjoyed that week away together. It was the first time we had spent so much time together since we were living at home as daft teenagers with your grandparents."

Chapter 4 – First Round of the Season

I didn't fancy starting back in a medal but it was arranged a few weeks later Ruby would come round one Saturday afternoon and I would book a game for about 3 pm when the course would be quiet and I would see if I could get my swing back. As the days passed I began to look forward and get excited about being out on the links again and experience that feeling of exhilaration I got when at the top of the hill, looking out on the city of Edinburgh and the view over the Firth of Forth towards North Berwick and over the sea to Elie.

I was out of practice about setting out on a round of golf and although I polished my shoes and checked the caddy car was working I didn't check my golf bag until about to tee up at the first. I then found the disgusting mummified remains of last year's BLT sandwich. I threw it out hastily, zipped that pocket shut and found a ball and tee elsewhere in the bag. I hit a few decent shots, sunk a couple of putts and was quite pleased I could still play a bit. Mind you that rescue club was hopeless; each shot seemed to put me in more trouble where a wedge was required to extricate me from an even worse position than I'd been in. I made a mental note to bin the club when I got home and to put a 4 iron back in the bag.

The Club House was empty when I went in for a drink at 6 30 - all the day golfers had long gone and the evening lounge lizards had yet to arrive. I had a chat with Jackie the steward, and asked what had been happening. "Och, not much, the usual you know. Bandits join the club, get a ridiculous handicap and win 3 medals in a row until the handicap committee catch up with them." "No scandal then?" "That lassie you used to go out with has got a new bloke" "What, Jenny?" "Aye that's the one. She's went blonde and this boy is a pro on the Challenger Tour. Hits the ball a mile, came up here and broke the course record-it's now 61 by the way." "OK, sorry I asked" having heard enough about Mr Perfect. "The only other thing to note is that Big Dan was disciplined and suspended for 6 months." "Oh! Tell me more about that." "Well it seems that he and the Hon. John fell out over some sort of building deal and at the Prize Giving Dinner. Big Dan got a bit drunk and when the Hon. John, as incoming captain gave his inaugural speech about the integrity of golf Big Dan stood up and called him a hypocrite and a fucking liar. There's now a court case and people are saying if Big Dan loses he is likely to have his membership withdrawn. That's all I know and I'm not taking sides." "What does Big Dan do these days because he was always up here?" I inquired. "Apparently he drinks down at the Murrayfield Hotel most nights but he is not in a good mood and his time there might be called too. There's a worry the business he built up over the last 40 years might go down the tubes."

I went back to my seat in the empty bar with my pint and tried to make sense of all of this information I'd been given. The last time I had seen these two protagonists they seemed friendly and played a healthy game to the best of their limited golfing abilities.

Chapter 5 – Big Dan in his cups

I knocked back my pint and wandered off to the Murrayfield Hotel taking the precaution to leave my car in the car park. The Hotel was quite busy with fans who had congregated for a Rugby 7s tournament which was being played this weekend at Murrayfield Stadium (or whatever it is called these days) which was just across the road.

I remembered there was a small bar at the back for locals as due to its proximity to the stadium the hotel often got swamped by once-in-a-lifetime visitors. There in the far corner sat Big Dan. He had a pint of Guinness well under way and a whisky keeping it company. He was alone, hunched over his mobile phone and exuding all sorts of subliminal messages that he wanted to be alone.

"Mind if I join you?" I opened. "Yes" came the terse reply without looking up.

"I might be able to help you?" I replied with as tantalising an offer as I could make. "If you've got £2 million leave it with me and fuck off" said Dan still apparently studying his phone. "Just give me a few minutes of your time Dan" I said, in a last throw. "I've always admired and respected you apart from these fucking awful golf clubs you play with."

He looked up. "Who are you again?" he said focussing his bleary eyes on me. "Jock from the golf club" I replied in the sure and certain knowledge I was the only member with such a forename. "Well I'm not allowed in the club at the moment and probably never again." "So I have just heard." "Where the fuck have you been this past miserable 12 months," said Dan exasperatedly.

I explained about my Dad and how today was my first round of golf at the club since I had seen him and the Hon. John playing together.

"Well a lot has changed since that day. I thought I had my big chance to get the biggest contract my firm had ever had. That John bastard had diversified and had taken on this school build but it was a difficult site and needed a bridge re-aligned to make maximum use of a valuable piece of land in the school's bourgeois catchment area. As you know about a quarter of Edinburgh kids go to private schools - one of the biggest proportions in the world. I know I sent my three there and a right lot of toffee-nosed bastards they've turned out. None of them has the remotest interest in taking over the firm from me. One of the girls did Art History and values Clarice fucking Cliff china at Sotheby's, the boy is in a heavy metal band in Berlin and the wee lassie paints her toenails and fuck knows what else up in her room all day on line and says she wants to be the next Kim Kardashian." "Does she have a big arse?" I enquired helpfully. Dan stopped and burst out laughing. There were almost tears running down his cheeks before he stopped. "Hey Jock sit down for a minute you always were a decent guy, but a bit of a fucking loser."

Chapter 6 – Disclosure

Over the next hour Big Dan told me how he thought he had a deal with Hon. John and put a lot of work into the project. Dan's company was to be a major subcontractor doing most of the school build so that one of Hon. John's companies would do the groundworks and the major civil engineering including re-alignment of the bridge and surrounding roads. Then at the last minute, Hon. John phoned and said he was bringing in another firm from outside - a nationally known building company but I could get some of the fitting out work to do towards the end of the project. I thought we had a deal but Hon. John said nothing had been put in writing. I got really angry but Hon. John said that was it take it or leave it and to let him know by close of play the next day.

"I went to see Terry Reilly for some legal advice," said Dan. "He was just a drunk," I replied. "Well I didn't realise it at the time but he said he would try and sort something out, the time limit passed and while he promised to sue the bastard for me he was killed the following week driving home to his fancy house in Cramond. He crashed his big Mercedes sports car into a wall and his post mortem showed he was four times the legal limit for drink."

"But you had a hand shake deal did you not?" "Yes but I was told it was his word, as a toff and a gentleman, against mine, as an ex labourer of Irish stock, who had once given a false name to the cops when I was caught under-age drinking when I was 17."

"What are you going to do?" I tried suing him but my new lawyers say prospects are poor and if I lose I will be ruined and meantime he is suing me for defamation on account of me calling him a liar and a hypocrite at that Club dinner when he was made captain. I'm not apologising to that twister." "Did you perchance agree a handshake deal on the 6th fairway on afternoon last July?" "Y-yes. How do you know?" I was there playing on my own." "I never saw you." "No I realised you two were engrossed and you would never have waved me through so I held back and only caught up again near the end when you won with that par putt on the 17th." "I don't believe this," gasped Dan. "The court case is coming up in two weeks' time - will you be a witness?" "Absolutely" I replied. "I've always preferred you to him. I wouldn't want any of your clubs even if you paid me but the Hon. John wouldn't sell me his putter." I replied, inscrutably.

"My wife says there are days when I'm closer to shooting my weight than my age."- Bob Hope

Dan and I had a bit of a session in the Hotel that night and I walked home the worse for wear minus my car. I did not get a good reception back home and no further offers of golfing respite therapy were forthcoming.

On Tuesday morning Ms Melissa Harper, an attractive young lawyer, appeared at my office on behalf of Dan's solicitors and took a statement from me. I am afraid I gawped at this woman who was immaculately turned out in a close fitting black suit and looked very professional. She had obviously got a statement from Big Dan and carefully asked me to tell my story, asking a few neutral questions to get things down in my own words and only intervened when

I seemed to stray from that which she considered relevant to the case. I was told that it was likely counsel would probably add my statement to the case papers and I might be asked to give evidence at the proof which was due to start the following Tuesday.

Chapter 7 – Cited to Court

Sure enough a citation arrived for me to attend the Court of Session in Parliament Square, Edinburgh, next to St Giles Cathedral for the proof. The accompanying papers told me to be at court for 9 30 am prompt on the Tuesday, but in the event I was put off until the next day. It was too late to go to work so I went home only to find both Mum and Dad fast asleep in the lounge. A dribble of saliva was dripping on to Dad's shirt but I wiped this away with a tissue and I put a cushion under Mum's head to stop her head rocking back too far on the low-backed chair. I tidied away the tea cups and plates from their sandwich lunch and went to look for a fresh white shirt to be ready for court the next day. I am afraid to say I rarely entered the laundry room and as I stretched to lift a shirt from a pile in the ironing basket, I kicked over my golf bag and a ball rolled out and went under the washing machine. Although I had kept on my membership at the Club I had cleared out my locker to save cash and indeed to let a more active member have the benefit of the facility. It was a particularly large clumsy tour bag which was alright on a trolley but totally awkward the rest of the time.

After a struggle using a wire coat-hanger, I got the ball back and was about to stuff it in the nearest pocket of the bag when I remembered the smelly sandwich that had been in there. I grabbed a yellow rubber glove of my Mum's that she seemed to spend a good portion of her life wearing and fished about in the pocket.

The remains of a fossilised apple emerged and various ball wrappers, receipts from the pro shop and a sticky corner of a Mar Bar to which was adhering a grubby piece of paper. For the first time I read this document entitled _HEADS OF AGREEMENT_ properly and realised the significance of it. I raked amongst the detritus of the golf bag pocket and selected another piece of paper and binned the rest. I rushed up the stairs and phoned Big Dan's lawyers.

"Can I speak to Ms Harper in litigation?" "Who's calling?" replied an indifferent voice. "Jock Kirkcaldy. I am a witness in the Court of Session building case that's going on this week." "Ms Harper is very busy just now," replied the voice with the same level and almost bored tone. "Look, this is urgent and could make all the difference to her case." I exclaimed. "Hang on then" said the receptionist in a voice which I knew was going to condemn me to a very long wait.

After an eternity a bright young voice came on the line "Mr Kirkcaldy are you still there? It's Ms Harper here." I gabbled out my story and must have sounded almost deranged but I could sense her sitting immaculately at her desk apparently giving me her full attention but able to consider many other things at the same time. "So you say you have documentary proof to back up what you told me last week?" she replied succinctly after I had run out of words. "It's very late in the day and I am about to meet counsel and then Mr Foulkes to discuss prospects and perhaps settlement". "You mean the Hon. John is falling on his sword?" "Far from it." she replied", but he has offered to forego some of fees he has incurred in the litigation." "I can't think that will go down well with Big Dan." I replied. "Perhaps not," she replied calmly", but clients often only see the issues clearly at the door of the court." "Do you not want to see this stuff?" I asked. "Can you scan it and e mail it to me?" "No I am afraid I am at home and don't have these facilities." "Then I think we must conclude this has all come too late Mr Kilmarnock," and she hung up. I was furious, not least for having my name confused with some West of Scotland town. I tried to phone Dan but his mobile was switched off.

I then heard my Mum shouting. Dad had fallen and for the next hour or so I was fully occupied getting him up, checking him over, phoning NHS 24 and seeing him into the ambulance with Mum. I wanted to come too but was told to stay back and clear up and have things ready for when he was discharged, which would likely be in a day or two. It took a while to tidy up the mess left by the paramedics and put dad's soiled clothes in the washing machine.

I looked at my watch. It was 9 20 and for the first time in about 5 hours I had time to reflect on the conversation I had had with Ms Harper.

I checked with Mum that she was staying over at the hospital and Dad was comfortable (i.e. not very well but not at the 'jump-leads' stage). I ran out of the house and drove off to the Murrayfield Hotel. There had been a Rotary Club event on and those patrons were leaving and milling about in the foyer as rain had started and would-be walkers were deciding to call taxis.

Chapter 8 – The Plan

I pushed through this dithering throng and searched for Big Dan but he was nowhere to be seen. "Has the Big Man been in tonight?" I asked the barman. "Aye but I had to put him out about 15 minutes ago as he got very drunk and just ended up babbling a lot of bad language. I hope the daft old bastard hasn't tried to drive home." I rushed out into the car park at the far corner found Big Dan slumped over the wheel of his Audi A8. I tried the door but it was locked and banged on the window without success. The manageress came out and shouted "Don't worry, I've called the police." Feverously I thought of the options - smash the window and drag him out? I tried the other doors to no avail but then tried the boot and it opened. I was able to pull down the seats and crawl into the passenger compartment. I popped the doors, then dragged Dan out of his car and poured him into mine. I retrieved his keys and briefcase, locked the Audi up and just managed to drive out of the car park and away just as I saw a marked police car hove into view.

I took Dan home to Mum's and laid him down in the spare room with his shoes and tie off and let him sleep in the recovery position. I got a blanket and slept fitfully in a bedside chair. Dan came to life, as I suppose he always did, about 6 am and after some re-assurance from me I got him to take a shower and made him some toast and coffee.

He told me that the meeting at the lawyer's office yesterday afternoon had been a disaster and both the advocate and that female solicitor had ganged up on him to settle which would involve him only having to bear half of Hon. John's legal expenses which together with his own would be about £150,000 instead of £350,000 if he went all the way and lost. He said he had stormed out when the lawyers said they would withdraw if he went on and said they would see him in court at 9 30 when they hoped things would be sorted out amicably.

I showed Dan the documents I had. Ms Harper had mentioned something about a phone call from you saying you sounded drunk and in any event it was too late to lodge them in process and even if they managed to do this Hon. John's lawyers would crucify me in court and suggest I had made the whole thing up. It took ages to talk Big Dan round but eventually I convinced him of a way forward and we set off in a taxi for court at 9 am.

Chapter 9 – Court of Session Proof

I left Big Dan to have a rowdy meeting with his lawyers where he sacked them. They said they had given an assurance to the other side the litigation would not proceed. Dan told them they had no authority to do so and told them to leave. Counsel suggested it would be better if he formally withdrew in court and give an explanation for so doing to the judge. Big Dan said he was not interested in his sensibilities and told him to get lost. There was some consternation in the other camp and a large red-faced senior counsel came over to Big Dan and told him his position was untenable. Big Dan told him he was going on and that he should cancel his lunch engagement and any others he had for the remainder of the week. In the meantime I had chatted up the Clerk and made up a list called an Inventory of Papers which Dan wanted to lodge. Finally a few minutes after 10 o'clock the judge walked in resplendent in his crimson Court of Session robes.

Big Dan was ready with a script which I had prepared for him drawing on my limited experience of court room law from 20 years ago. He stood to address the judge but was ignored and instead he asked the defence advocate to speak. "Mr Uphall, would you be good enough to explain the position to the court."

"Thank you, My Lord. This action has been vigorously contested over the last 18 months and yesterday afternoon it appeared settlement discussions had resolved matters. Counsel had taken the opportunity to discuss matters further when another case which had priority proceeded to proof yesterday. I was given to understand by my learned friend Mr O'Brien that our proposals were acceptable, and I was somewhat taken aback to find my learned friend had been summarily dismissed by the Pursuer, Mr Foulkes, and was precluded by his former client from explaining the position to Your Lordship. As Your Lordship well knows, these courts cannot function without the highest level of integrity between practitioners and when an indication that settlement has been reached it would be contrary to public policy and the smooth running of these courts to allow parties to change their minds at this late stage."

"Thank you for that helpful explanation, Mr Uphall, now Mr Foulkes you do understand the difficult position you are in?"

"All too well, My Lord. Until yesterday afternoon I was assured by Mr O'Brien and his solicitor Ms Harper who I see are nervously watching from the back of Your Lordship's court that I had a winnable case and recent evidence which had come into my possession strengthened my hand. Indeed further evidence was disclosed to my lawyers yesterday afternoon which they chose not to investigate and to refer to obliquely at our meeting, no doubt to protect their backs, but at the same time they were less than frank with me. I was told I should settle on the humiliating terms offered by my opponent and when I refused it was left for me to speak finally with my advisers this morning knowing I had either to accept the offer or go it alone, and it is the latter I chose to do. Mr O'Brien far exceeded his position in the case to speak to his friend Mr Uphall in such terms.

I appreciate there is a case involving a well- known litigant *Mowbray v Valentine* 2004 SC 21 and indeed the more recent Inner House authority *Mazur v Primrose and Gordon WS* [2015] CSIH 8 which may be argued against me but there is no inconvenience to the court here. I am sure Your Lordship fully expected this case to go on today and as far as I can see witnesses who spent a fair time waiting yesterday are here today. I am sure my friend Mr Uphall has his case at his fingertips in a way which Mr O' Brien was not prepared to face up to. Subject to some small preliminary matters I am prepared to proceed to proof."

"Err, thank you Mr Foulkes," said the judge clearly rattled by this large, roughly hewn man's eloquence and knowledge of the law and procedure. Mr O'Brien protested but the judge's mind was made up and he ordered the proof to proceed.

Big Dan then lodged an Inventory of extra documentary productions which he explained were things his ex-lawyers didn't want to use, but he felt were helpful to his case. It had cost me a fortune but I managed to create a few copies of these documents and made up bundles for Hon. John's lawyer and the judge.

I noticed Mr O' Brien hand this bundle to a tall short-sighted man behind him, presumably to examine. Although he had lost the first skirmish, O'Brien oozed confidence as he knew his opponent was a self-made and taught man who would not be able to use a script all the way through the case. "My first witness is from the list lodged last week by my ex-lawyer, I call Mr Jock Kirkcaldy!"

I took the oath then explained who I was and described how I had come across the parties golfing and how they shook hands in the middle of the 6th hole then proceeded to play competitively until the 17th green where Mr Foulkes appeared to win the game after which the two men strode off amicably to the 19th hole.

"You're just making this up and it is a tissue of lies constructed by yourself and Mr Foulkes to try and help him wriggle out of earlier lies he told," opened up the red-faced Mr O'Brien, in full bullying senior counsel mode when he rose to cross-examine.

I turned to the judge "My Lord I don't think that is a fair statement; I have not long taken to oath and I have been accused of all manner of things, some of which I cannot possibly know and without any facts to back up these offensive suggestions."

"He's right you know, Mr O'Brien. If this is to be your line you need to lay proper foundations." "I'm obliged My Lord," lied O'Brien and I permitted myself a wan smile.

O'Brien was clearly not used to such an early setback and he shuffled his papers for about 10 seconds no doubt to try and unsettle me as he frantically regrouped.

"How can you possibly say that you followed the match between my client and Mr Foulkes on the 17th of July last year?"

Chapter 10 – The Rabbit from the Hat

"It was the day my father sustained a serious stoke from which he has not totally recovered." "I am sorry to hear that." said the bully, shedding a few crocodile tears. "How can you equate your father's stroke to what did or did not take place on the golf course?"

"My meeting finished early that day as I thought it might so I went straight to Silverfield Golf Club and teed off about 3 pm." "How can you be so sure?" said O'Brien innocently, but beginning to lay a trap. "Well, I bought a drink and a sandwich at the Pro Shop and I think you will find the receipt in that bundle you handed to the gentleman behind you." This produced a bit of consternation and the short-sighted gent was suddenly supplemented by a smart young woman in a dark suit who looked like Ms Harper's identical twin. After much fumbling the copy document was found and His Lordship was directed to the appropriate production number in his bundle. I could sense that in addition to value of the document which was now in evidence, O'Brien was horrified to find that his opponent had not only lodged documents but had done so in the proper way with all items numbered for ease of reference. It was all in the Rules of Court but usually that was where O'Brien scored over principled but chaotic lay opponents.

"Why was this just discovered yesterday?" I have only played one quick game of golf since my father's stroke and I did not tidy out my golf bag until I tripped over it in the laundry room when I was searching for a fresh shirt to wear today at court." I replied sweetly. "Do tell us more!" said O'Brien hoping my glib answers would be my undoing. "Well in the event, on the 17th of July last year, I didn't eat the whole sandwich I purchased, and only discovered the remains when looking for a golf ball the other week. When I tripped over the bag yesterday it reminded me to give it a thorough clean out and I found this among other things that included a dead apple and a piece of a Mars Bar. Your copy won't show it but the original of that receipt is sticky to the touch."

"Anything else you find in this Pandora's Box?" "Well yes there was. When I caught up with the match at the 6th I tidied up the tee box which seemed to have been attacked by seagulls and I picked up this piece of paper entitled *HEADS OF AGREEMENT*. It looked important but I didn't read it and stuck it in my bag, and in the ensuing emergency I forgot all about until I came across it yesterday. I think this is his number 19 in that bundle, Mr O'Brien I added helpfully."

There was more frantic fumbling from the other side and suddenly O'Brien shouted at me "This is a complete fabrication!" "It may be inconvenient to you and contrary to what you have been led to believe but I find it objectionable that you should accuse me of a serious crime without any proof."

"Mr O'Brien?" said the judge with a raised eyebrow. "I apologise, My Lord; I withdraw the question."

"Perhaps," said the judge wisely, "this would be a convenient time to adjourn for you to take instructions on this matter." "Quite so, My Lord " said O'Brien sadly realising the judge had correctly assessed this piece of evidence had come like a bolt out of the blue.

We resumed about half an hour later. I kept well put of the way of Big Dan although I know he was desperate to speak to me, but this would have been contrary to the rules since I was in the middle of my evidence, and would have given O'Brien a stick with which to discredit me.

Instead his tone was completely different, and he restricted himself to confirming that at no time had I heard what either man said during the part of the golf match I witnessed. Somehow I did manage to get in that the last 18 months had been a bit of a blur trying to hold down a responsible job, support my mother and help care for my father including changing nappies several times a day.

Fortunately Big Dan could think of no questions to ask me. He had forgotten to ask me about the receipt and the paper earlier but O'Brien had done this for us which was much more effective and hopefully compelling.

As I left the witness box and went to find a seat at the rear of the court, I noticed Mr Uphall and Ms Harper were still there. I just looked straight through her and took a seat some distance away.

Big Dan gave evidence next and confirmed there had been a handshake deal which he understood was sufficient under Scots Law. He had always respected the Hon. John although they had never been friends and understood his firm to be good at what they did. He had been taken aback at the way he had been dumped from the contract, and appalled at the ruthless way he had been treated for someone he had always understood to be a gentleman; one who had the benefit of a much better education and start to life that he had. It was evident that in some way Big Dan had annoyed him and the Hon. John seemed to then set out to obliterate him from the commercial world, despite the fact that apart from this one contract, the companies worked in different fields in the building world.

O'Brien tried all his tactics to break and unsettle Big Dan but having used most of them on me Big Dan knew the tack to take and even sought help from the judge when the questioning again went over the top.

"Am I entitled to object to my friend's question?" said Big Dan sweetly. "Indeed you are, Mr Foulkes." "I withdraw the question," said O'Brien. "Thank you, Mr O'Brien, please move on," said the judge as if hinting he was getting bored with Hon. John's case.

After a long day in court Big Dan and I met as agreed in the back room at the Murrayfield Hotel, each of us having ensured we were not followed.

Chapter 11 – Proof Day 2

Our case was closed and we awaited Hon. John's evidence the next day.

I agreed to come back to court and sit at the rear and Big Dan got Janice from his office to discreetly run messages between us.

"I think that document I found is key" I told Dan; he had never seen it until I showed him it but it echoed the terms of the deal he agreed with Hon. John on the day. Fortunately Dan had given his ex-lawyers a statement which had been lodged with the court before I had re-discovered the piece of paper.

The next day the Hon. John appeared smartly but simply dressed and was extremely polite and respectful to the judge as O'Brien led him through his evidence of denial. He said how he knew Dan through the building trade and as a fellow member of Silverfield. They had not been rivals as Dan had worked on small domestic contracts whereas the Hon. John had worked locally as well as abroad, and had contracts with multi-nationals including in Afghanistan. He had no doubt Dan was competent at his level, but the school contract was a tricky one located in a tight site. As the local authority had heaped all the risk on to the contractors, it was important to have experienced firms employed at all levels of the job, and in the final analysis Mr Foulkes' firm was not at that level at the present time. He had merely sounded out Dan's willingness and knowledge and decided against offering a written contract which was the way he did business.

It was Dan's turn to cross examine. "You offered me the job and we shook hands on it."

"Is that a question, Mr Foulkes?" replied Hon. John calmly. "Of course it is, John. We had a deal, didn't we?" "No we did not. It is not my style to shake hands in the middle of a game of golf. At the level I conduct business I sound people out, discuss the options with my colleagues then ask our lawyers to make a formal offer in writing. In that way I avoid court room situations like this which arise out of misunderstandings or downright dishonesty." "Well which is it to be here?" asked Dan. "You're not telling the truth." "What about the *HEADS OF AGREEMENT* document then?" responded Dan changing tack and handing the document to the Hon. John. "Well, it's obviously a complete grubby forgery put together by your drinking companion." The words stung back despite the calm clipped delivery of the witness. "It's crumpled and sticky and there are typing mistakes, and the page layout falls far short of what my secretaries would produce." "What if you typed it yourself?" pressed Dan. "Certainly not!" retorted John discarding the plastic wrapped document on to the top of the witness box. "I'm not finished with that document yet! Take these rubber gloves and remove the paper from the plastic covering please." said Dan firmly.

"Just stop there!" O'Brien growled jumping to his feet. "I object to this futile questioning." "Well Mr Foulkes, what do you have to say?" said the judge in a neutral tone. "My Lord, the witness has accused Mr Kirkcaldy of fabricating evidence and I am entitled to challenge that statement." "Mr O'Brien?" "Well My Lord, if the pursuer wishes to attempt to assert some sort of probity to this document he should have had it examined by an expert and lodged their report."

"I don't need to do that, My Lord," responded Dan. I just want to ask some simple questions which the witness should be able to answer. We don't need to produce an expert to say whether the sticky bits are Mars Bar or a Snickers." said Dan testily. "Very well I shall repel the objection. Would you like to take the document out please, Mr McDermid and we can continue, thank you." said the judge.

The Hon. John did as he was told but tried to fight back in a small way by exaggerating the sticky bits.

"Would you please hold the document up to the light, sir and tell me what you see apart from the typing and the sticky bits?" said Dan. "What am I supposed to be looking for?" replied the Hon. John in as level a voice as he could manage." "Your personal watermark." "That must have been forged too" replied the Hon. John. "Thank you" said Dan and sat down smartly.

From my seat at the rear of the court I could sense the tension of the moment. It was what had been left unsaid that was so effective. O'Brien was clearly flustered at this revelation and was slow to rise to his feet. "Any re-examination?" said the judge in the same neutral voice, but I sensed there was a little edge to this remark which would look innocent enough if read in any subsequent transcript of the proceedings. O'Brien took the document from his client and studied it for a full 20 seconds. "What can you say about this watermark, Mr McDermid?" said O'Brien. It was the best the QC could do in the circumstances as he was in danger of the case turning against him. "Well it must be part of the forgery or perhaps a stolen piece of my stationery was used as a plan to force me to allow Mr Foulkes to become involved in this tricky project." "Thank you," said O'Brien and sat down. He clearly wanted to distance himself from this sticky chapter of the evidence.

No further witnesses were called so the judge said "Gentlemen, it is nearly time for luncheon. I shall hear your submissions at 2 o'clock." Then he rose, we all bowed and scraped and we adjourned.

Chapter 12 – Final Submissions

I waited for Dan to gather his stuff and come out of court, and as we went off in search of a sandwich we could already see the Hon. John and O'Brien marching swiftly to and fro in Parliament Hall in the time honoured fashion to avoid being overheard. It was clear from the tone of their exchanges and gestures that all was not well despite the fact that the each turned smartly in unison when they reached one end of the hall or the other.

We went across the road for a tactics chat to Deacon Brodie's Tavern, named after an infamous town counsellor and criminal. By the time I brought two half pints and two whiskies plus a couple of filled rolls back to our corner table Dan was depressed. "I hoped that watermark thing would have broken him! It was a real bonus when you spotted it this morning." "Don't worry, their reactions were not lost on the judge when you revealed that piece of evidence. I bet O'Brien's had a note from the Hon. John at some point on notepaper like that. Did you see how he backed off the whole thing" I said trying to cheer Dan up. "Let me tidy up your closing remarks. Keep it short. Play the wee guy who's not as stupid as he looks." "Oh thanks very much, Jock," responded Dan as he knocked back the remains of both drinks and rose to go back across to the court.

Dan followed my advice and pitched his speech just right as the simple man who assumed he had a deal from the handshake of an Honourable man and not only did he feel wronged at being dumped from the build, but he had spent money, made plans in anticipation and had been disappointed both personally and professionally and had incurred the various losses set out.

O'Brien was his usual blustering self but I detected a hint of holding back. Nevertheless he made all the points; we were liars, the document was a fake, the deal had never happened and quite frankly Mr Foulkes was kidding himself if he imagined being in a building consortium with the Hon John McDermid's internationally renowned firm.

"Thank you gentlemen for these succinct submissions. I was minded to take the case away for a few weeks to *avizandum,* but essentially the matter boils down to one of credibility and reliability. I shall adjourn for about half an hour to consider the evidence again in light of your helpful speeches then I hope to deliver an *ex tempore* judgment."

"What did all that mean?" said Dan after the judge had departed for his chambers. "It means he has made up his mind and can't be bothered to write up a full long decision but will give us a quickie instead", I replied giving Dan the benefit of my knowledge of the modern court. "Fuck! That must mean we've lost and the toff wins as usual!" wailed Dan. "Not necessarily so. I don't think the other side liked it either. I am sure the Hon. John wants something in copperplate which he can pin on the Club Notice Board."

Chapter 13 – The Judgment

Half an hour later, after being alerted by the clerk of court, we were back in our places and bowing and scraping in unison as His Lordship ascended the bench.

"Thank you gentlemen, I am grateful at the expeditious way in which you conducted this litigation. Business disputes are like family cases in that sometimes the court has to become involved, but thereafter parties are likely to bump into each other and have to develop some sort of ongoing relationship. After all, Scotland is a small country and you are both likely to come across each other at some stage – and you are both members of the same golf club. As is invariably the case in litigation the court ultimately has to try and resolve competing testimonies. The *onus* rests with the Pursuer and if I am not satisfied with that case on a balance of probabilities the action fails as it does if I accept the Defender's case. Mr McDermid comes from a distinguished family and a business which has spanned the generations. Mr Foulkes Company is more modest but built up from scratch. One must look at the facts. Mr McDermid denies an agreement was ever reached that day on the golf course, and gives reasons why that should be and says the case against him is a complete fabrication borne out of revenge for not achieving what was never on offer. On the other hand, I found Mr Foulkes and Mr Kirkcaldy's evidence to be plausible and while the late arrival of Mr Kirkcaldy's affidavit into the proceedings, and the even later disclosure of the Heads Of Agreement document was the subject of criticism, I found that body of evidence compelling and difficult to imagine as a cunning conspiracy complete with forgery. Accordingly I find the Pursuer's case both credible and reliable, not only do I prefer that evidence, but I regret to say I totally disbelieved the Defender. I find in the Pursuer's favour for the sum sued, namely £50,000 and I take it Mr O'Brien you accept expenses follow success?" "Yes, My Lord" said O'Brien dismally. "Well Mr Foulkes, submit your account to the Court for taxation and you will also be paid your reasonable expenses of this litigation."

We were elated. Dan and I had a night on the town. Next day we learned the Hon. John had relinquished the captaincy of Silverfield and resigned his membership of the club. The way seemed clear for Big Dan to return to Silverfield and play with those expensive, but to my eyes tawdry golf clubs.

Play Golf Not War

Chapter 1 – The Old Man

My father had an odd relationship with golf. He was good at it, and as a scratch man in his prime much better than me with my 12 handicap. He had been club champion 5 times in a row in the 1950s and won again in 1967, the year of my birth and finally in 1971, though he was runner up 4 other times. On the other hand at times he seemed depressed despite this ability, and on occasion would storm out of the house to play golf alone, and my mother, who seemed very accommodating, would assure us Dad just needed time to himself on the golf course.

He was born in 1921 and when he left school in 1939 war loomed. He had been born in Leith, the port of Edinburgh and lived with his docker father, mother and three other children in a tenement flat down near The Shore. He used to point it out to me if we took a shortcut through the narrow cobbled streets past Beldam Lascar Packing's premises, which had occupied the ground floor in Queen Charlotte Street.

There was some controversy, still fanned to this day by the writer Irvine Welsh, that Leith should never have become part of the City of Edinburgh local authority area in 1920. It did, and one of the beneficiaries was my father, who as the cleverest boy in his primary school class won a scholarship to the Royal High School where Sir Walter Scott and many other dignitaries had been pupils.

"Golf, like the measles should be caught young, for if postponed to riper years, the results may be serious."- P G Wodehouse

So in 1933 he walked up Leith Walk towards the imposing Greco-Roman school building built beside Calton Hill with fine views of Edinburgh Castle and Arthur's Seat. There were boys there from other feeder schools around Edinburgh and he soon mixed in and thrived on the teaching, some of the sports and the cadets. He became friendly with a few of the posh boys whose parents paid fees, many of whom had attended the Royal High Primary School (which had opened in 1931) beforehand and had formed close friendships with them despite their aptitude for rugby which my father never achieved.

He had become interested in watching old men playing golf on Leith Links where The Honourable Company of Edinburgh Golfers (HCEG) had played from 1744 until they decamped to Musselburgh, before settling at Muirfield twenty miles away in East Lothian in 1891.

On the rudimentary links which remained at Leith, my father learned to play with hickory clubs, woods with wooden heads and irons, or cleeks as he called them with unforgiving thin soles and flat backs. He even said he started playing with gutty balls which were solid and give stinging feedback to the hands on a cold day if you didn't middle the ball with the club. Dad always said Haskell-type rubber balls were a doddle to play by comparison although their bounce near the green made it difficult to lay the ball dead to the hole as was possible with the gutty and greens which back in the day were not so close-cropped.

Dad played a bit of cricket which left him with a shortish brisk swing which I have inherited, often with

disastrous consequences. He did tell me this early
exposure to windy links golf led to him playing most
of his shots with a low drawing right to left, flat,
penetrating trajectory but this was to change. He never
had any formal lessons and apart from some tips from
the old men on Leith Links he drew most of his early
golfing knowledge from a book his father gave him for
his 10th birthday – 'Essentials of Golf' by Abe Mitchell
who was reputed to be the best striker of the ball in
his day in the 1920s. Abe was 4th in the 1914, 1920 and
1929 Open Championships, 5th in 1925 and still made
the top 10 in 1932 and 1933 - a total of 8 top 10s in
17 appearances. Dad was also able to tell me Abe taught
Sam Ryder to play golf in the 1920s and by way of a
thank you Ryder had Abe cast as the figure to adorn the
top of the Ryder Cup.

In later years at the Royal High, Dad's golfing abilities
were recognised and he played in a small golf section
with about 20 other boys out of a school roll of about
700. This facility enabled him to play many of the
courses in the Edinburgh area and stretching down
the coast to North Berwick. He particularly appreciated
the ever turning layout of Bruntsfield, its fine views and
magnificent greens but ultimately thought Silverfield
was more affordable, and through his Latin teacher
Mr Ure, or 'Badger' (as he was universally called behind
his back), he became a junior member in 1935.

Dad did a paper round (or sometimes two) before
setting off for school, and gradually, a club or two at a
time, he purchased a set of Ben Sayers 'Crown' clubs
from Thornton's Sports Shop in Princes Street. Eventually
after a few years he had a full set. These were four woods
comprising a Driver, Brassie, Spoon and Baffy, along
with eight irons comprising Cleek, Driving Iron, Mid
Iron, Mashie Iron, Mashie, Mashie Niblick, Niblick,
Jigger and 2 putters. One of the putters had a normal loft

while the other was a 'special' or 1 iron putter with more loft for approach shots over fringes on to greens. Dad loved these clubs with their 'Kinghorn' Tacky Grips made by the Bridge of Weir Leather Co Ltd. He was devastated when they gave up making these grips in the 1960s and eventually he had to settle for rubber Golf Pride 'Tour Wrap' grips mixed with cord which I must say I found harsh on my hands, but still use the faux leather wrap style of grip myself.

Golf was not central to the Royal High curriculum of English, Maths, Latin, French or German and Sciences with lots of rugby and cricket thrown in. However the class of 1933 was a classic one for golfers, and soon my father had teamed up with Davie Spowart who came from Portobello and played at Musselburgh Old Golf Club, Brian Peden who came from Oxgangs and played at the quirky and sometimes impossibly steep Lothianburn course situated on the South side of the city nestling against the Pentland Hills. These three scholarship boys were joined by 'Posh' Johnny Romanes, whose father was a member of the well-known Princes Street shop Romanes & Paterson dynasty. Posh railed against this nickname and since he was already a very accomplished golfer and junior champion at Bruntsfield, the lads settled on the nickname of Jock.

Chapter 2 – The Royal High School Golf Team 1938-39

This quartet did well in a variety of tournaments in their last few years at school but took things to a new level when they won the Lothian Schools Foursomes Cup which was played each year over Edinburgh's spectacular Braid Hills layout. Back in the day the Cup was almost as prestigious as the Men's Foursomes which continues to this day at Braid Hills with competing teams playing for the Evening Dispatch Trophy.

In their final year at school, after exams were out of the way at the end of May, the boys played a rigorous round of matches over successive nights. First they saw off George Watson's College then in the second round beat Fettes College where Tony Blair was later a pupil, and the fictional spy James Bond was said to have been educated.

Their sister school Loretto was the boys' next scalp leading to the dream final against Royal High' s deadly rivals George Heriot's School. The match over 2 rounds was very close with all games being settled by the odd hole. As backmarkers, it fell to my father and Jock to try to win their match and the competition. The game ran right up to the end where the match was all square on the 18th tee. As the weaker player it fell to my Dad to tee off towards the uphill fairway, and into the prevailing wind, with a tiny target to locate on a vestigial fairway surrounded by trouble. It was not a long hole, but there was still about 50 feet of height to climb and a short stretch of fairway to a small green ahead. As opposed to my Dad's low shots Jock hit a towering approach with a wedge and the players scrambled up the slope to ascertain where these blind shots had landed. Jock's ball had landed stiff beside the pin leaving Dad with an easy putt. Their rival's shot which seemed quite promising had flown the green and was in rough some distance away. My Dad said that was just as well as he had been very nervous the longer the match went on and how tight it had become. Ascending on to the 18th green at the Braids was daunting at the best of times as you feel on top of the world with the ground falling away on all sides and a magnificent 360 degree view of Edinburgh and it surroundings. Dad had two shots to win and with shaky hands sunk what proved to be a straight 3 foot putt.

He and his colleagues were feted when they returned to School with the Cup, and had to give a small speech about their success at Assembly in the oval-shaped, hard-benched auditorium. It seemed for a brief moment golf had pushed the other school sports off the front page.

Dad and his team mates soon left School and had plans for the future but as the summer progressed uncertainty and the threat of war loomed ever closer over Europe. Jock was due to go to Oxford University to read law, while Dad applied to join the Civil Service inspired no doubt by the building of the art deco Scottish Office's headquarters at St Andrew's House directly across from his School. Davie Spowart was going to crew his father's fishing boat and perhaps study book-keeping in his spare time. Brian Peden was all set to join the Bank of Scotland and hope to work his way up the tree to becoming a branch manager, a position held by his father in Morningside, a wealthy Edinburgh suburb.

Chapter 3 – One Last Round
before thrashing Hitler

The 3rd of September 1939 changed all that and the boys hastily organised a game of golf which took place at Jock's home course of Bruntsfield on 18th September. Jock had just returned from his family's grouse shoot up near Dalwhinnie. Dad said he and his pals each received telegrams sent from Pitlochry inviting them to the game and ensuring they wore suits and ties when arriving at the club.

The boys' plans had changed radically; Davie and Dad were going to join the Royal Navy due to their love of the sea and fishing in the Firth of Forth, Jock was bound for the Royal Scots like his father and grandfather before him, while Brian was keen to join the Royal Air Force and become a pilot.

Time was short that day as all four had a lot to do before attending at recruitment centres so it was agreed they would play a foursomes match with the teams as they were in the Schools' Cup, namely Jock and Dad versus Brian and Davie. Despite quizzing him a few times Dad actually could remember little of the game. He put it down to them all being preoccupied with World events. Jock played some majestic shots as usual which was just as well. Dad said he played poorly as did the others but somehow Dad was sure it was due to some sleight of hand by Jock, as the game finished all square. They had all turned 18 that year so were able to go into the bar once jackets and ties were adorned. Dad specifically remembered Jock buying them all a dram of Haig's whisky which Dad thought awfully daring having previously just supped a few pints of Light beer. His Dad had warned him off the Heavy 80/- ale until he was a proper man, i.e. twenty one.

Jock had to report the following day to Redford Barracks on the South side of Edinburgh as per his call up papers, whereas Brian wasn't due to attend at East Fortune airfield in East Lothian until the start of October. On 25 September Davie and Dad took the train to North Queensferry just over the Forth Bridge. As they crossed over the River Forth Dad remembered Davie getting him to stand up to try and see where Robert Donat had hidden among the girders during a particularly exciting scene from Hitchcock's '39 Steps', scenes from which had been filmed on the bridge a few years before.

It was a 2 mile walk from the station to the Dockyard but as they drew near they realised they were not the only young men with a 9.30 appointment. It was a dreich, cold day and a steady drizzle often broke out into something even wetter. They joined a queue of similar young men mostly in raincoats and bunnets from which strong clouds of tobacco smoke issued. It was like the scene when Dad had queued at Hampden to watch an international football match.

It was about 1.30 before Dad and Davie managed to get undercover, and another 20 minutes before they were seen. After checking out their particulars they were ushered into a long corridor with screened areas where they were asked to strip to their pants and had a full medical examination. It was then Dad realised something was up as Davie quickly moved on to the next phase and was soon lost to view. Meantime Dad said it was both worrying and humiliating as he was rechecked by a more senior doctor then by another elderly gent whom the others referred to as 'Professor'. Shortly afterwards he was led into a small quiet room and left for about an hour until the door burst open and another doctor he had not seen previously came in flanked by the matron and a young nurse whom Dad could not help noticing was very attractive. How he remembered that detail goodness knows, because shortly afterwards he was told that he had 'TB' (Tuberculosis) and would have to attend at the Sanatorium at Craigmillar in Edinburgh forthwith.

Chapter 4 – Dad's Disgrace

There were no ambulances available but Dad was told to get a bus or train back to Edinburgh as soon as possible and ask for Ward 9 at the Hospital. He was told to sit away from others if at all possible and keep his scarf over his mouth.

Dad had to buy a return ticket and after getting off at Haymarket he caught a bus to Craigmillar where he found the staff were expecting him. He was not the only youth who ended up there that day after being rejected, but Dad was too engrossed in his own shock and sorrow; shock about the diagnosis and sorrow and not being able to join Davie and the other lads.

As he had left Rosyth dockyard he sensed the soldiers in the guard-box knew he was a reject. Then just as he left one shouted "Flat feet was it, coward!" "Fuck off!" retorted Dad. "It's TB, would you like me to breathe over you so that I can have your second opinion?"

Over the next few months Dad reflected over the last few years. His family did live in a small flat in a crowded tenement and he wasn't the first in his street with TB. Jeanie a sickly wee lassie down the street had died of it the previous year aged 9, the poor soul. Dad had been coughing over the summer but put it down to smoking too many Woodbine cigarettes. He realised that he didn't particularly enjoy them but everyone smoked back then especially film stars, football players and golfers whom Dad most admired. He was released in March 1940 and was able to get a job as a filing clerk in the Civil Service at St Andrew's House, from where he could see boys trooping up the road towards the Royal High School. He recognised a few of them but kept out of their way as he didn't want to go into long explanations why he wasn't in the forces like all normal young men.

Dad also did shifts at night as an Air Raid Warden, but that uniform fooled no one who took a close look at the youthful face directing them to safety or walking home after a night on Calton Hill searching for fires from incendiary bombs. He hated it all, and spent most of his spare time lying in bed at home depressed.

Chapter 5 – Wartime Golf

One day towards the end of 1940 Dad received a letter from the Secretary of Silverfield Golf Club sympathising with his rejection from the forces, hoping he was better and wondering if he could help him run a small committee since most of the members were elsewhere and some of the older ones had left town to avoid the bombing.

Reluctantly Dad agreed to help and one Saturday afternoon, with some trepidation, went to see Captain Brown MC. He had had a distinguished First World War as one of McCrae's Battalion of recruits which contained footballers from Heart of Midlothian FC and Raith Rovers, two of the clubs where players volunteered early in that war long before conscription came about. Many of the volunteers had been killed and survivors, especially decorated ones were held in high regard in Edinburgh between the Wars.

"Ah, Kirkcaldy, do come in and sit down" said Captain Brown to my father when he had knocked and entered the Secretary's room on command. Captain Brown was from another era and could recollect seeing Ben Sayers and Andrew Kirkcaldy, both esteemed professional golfers in their day, play the inaugural match over the new Silverfield links in 1896. The Captain recalled Ben Sayers as being a small man who played with a very long shafted driver called a Dreadnought after the great warships of that era, and Andrew Kirkcaldy having a bit of a temper. Kirkcaldy prevailed in the match when Ben's driving went a bit haywire. He complained about the sand in the bunkers being claggy and quite unlike the white stuff at North Berwick which had probably been purloined from nearby Dirleton beach. "Any relation?" asked the Captain hopefully. "Not as far as I know sir," replied my father. "Never mind. I hear that you learned from the best down at Leith Links and partnered young Romanes to win the Schools Cup last year, said the Captain.

Tea was brought in by the steward's daughter and the Captain set out his plans to keep as much of the course going throughout the War. "Got to keep up morale, young man!" boomed the Captain. Dad confessed however that he did not take in all of what was said at the meeting as his mind wandered to the shapely figure and red wavy hair of the steward's daughter. "I married that lassie after the War, she's your Mum!" That revelation had been a shock to me as I always assumed Mum been white-haired from birth. Later on in one of our last conversations I shared this thought with Dad. Although he was very poorly by this time he laughed for quite a while then whispered to me, "it was you being the late bairn that made her hair grow white - that and greetin' non-stop for 18 months. Yer still a grumpy bugger sometimes." "Well that must come from you," I replied coolly. "I'm trying to tell you why I am what I am", said Dad testily.

Chapter 6 – Captain Brown

Dad said he Captain Brown was a hard taskmaster and soon found he was doing all the Secretary's work, such as it was. Doris, the typist had gone off to join the Women's Land Army and none of the lady members could be persuaded to fill the post so dad had to learn on an ancient Remington machine. When the Captain said a letter was a really important one he didn't want any mistakes and would squint at the proffered page at an angle to see if there were any tell-tale signs of rub-outs. Dad said this apprenticeship proved invaluable as he rose in the Civil Service ranks post War. As Private Secretary to the Secretary of State for Scotland for example, his typing prowess was regularly used when the Minister wanted a clear note sent to one of his colleagues without Dad's bosses seeing it.

After a few bomb raids in the Edinburgh area and in the general panic after Dunkirk, Emergency Measures came into play. Rolls of barbed wire were strewn across fairways at regular intervals to prevent German troops landing gliders and light aircraft. Silverknowes, a relatively new course down on the Firth of Forth was partially dug up and potatoes were planted. When the Captain heard of this he replied "Thank God some of our holes are built on stony ground!"

I had to accompany the Captain when a Land Resources team came to visit the course. "It all looks very lush" said Mr Millington a tall urbane, recently retired civil servant whom I knew a little from work but doubted if he knew me. "Ah well," said the captain," I am sorry to disappoint you but looks can be deceiving. They had to import some soil from Fife to cover the rocky terrain when they built the course 40 odd years ago. We had to use tough fescue grass as on the high parts of the course it is very exposed and the grass doesn't grow much between October and March. Sometimes we have to close the top holes in the winter and often the lower part is flooded. We had plans about 10 years ago to improve the drainage, plant trees to curb the wind as well as suck up the moisture. As you know at the far end is an old quarry where Craigleith sandstone was mined to face up the houses in the New Town. They left an awful mess and some of the ground isn't very stable after a heavy shower of rain." Mr Millington let these words sink in and turned to Mr Mackenzie, an elderly farmer who presumably had been brought along for his tattie growing expertise. "What do you think Willie?" "It's just utter shite sir, if you don't mind saying. They've got the wrong grass and there would be nothing for sheep and cattle to see out the winter on these fields let alone grow crops. These fancy boys have let the whins abound and the best thing that can happen to them is for the Jerries to drop a few incendiaries on the whole lot." "Well Captain, I think that is a No at least for the moment, but we'll keep in touch. You will remember when we thought the last War would be over by Christmas, but this time we have a long way to go after Dunkirk. I hate to say it but we could do with the Yanks joining in." "They weren't that great the last time," replied the Captain, "but we could certainly do with their where-with-all now."

Millington turned round to leave then suddenly stared at my father. "Don't I know you from somewhere, young man?" "Y-yes sir" replied my father. I am a clerk/messenger at St Andrew's House and use to take mail to your office. I had hoped to join the Navy but they found out I had TB." "Bad show," said Millington "still make sure you get some golf in and think yourself lucky." Those words like other wartime exchanges stuck in my father's head for the rest of his life.

Actually there was very little time for golf in between looking after his mother and younger brothers, working during the day and fire-spotting at night. Once Dad said he had some spare time to play but found himself falling asleep as he walked down a fairway. His low drawing shots often got caught up in the barbed wire and one time he sustained a nasty cut on his right hand which went septic. Seventy years later you could still see the scar on the back of his liver-spotted hand where the laceration ran from the web between his thumb and forefinger. "Aye it was a right drunk old doctor that stitched me up but fortunately the nurse sorted things out wi' poultices when it went all pussy" reminisced my father one time - too much information!

Worse was to follow after the Battle of Britain in the late summer of 1940. German bombers turned their attention the following year to areas of strategic interest they thought would be less well protected - like Clydebank. There was some bombing in and around Edinburgh and Rosyth, and one night a Heinkel bomber went off course, possibly due to mechanical difficulties. Anyway it shed its load of bombs over Silverfield in a vain attempt to gain enough height to clear the Pentland Hills, but crashed about 20 miles away.

The Captain summoned me the next day and along with police and army officers survey the damage. The 9th hole was worst affected with a great crater dwarfing the bunkers which previously had protected the green.

Now with a makeover from that hitherto little-known golf architect, Adolf Hitler, this hole had become virtually impregnable.

While the course was re-opened soon after, many of the older members which was most of them, simply by-passed the 9th green. Dad persevered usually with disastrous consequences due to his low ball flight. Even if he cleared the Hitler bunker he could never stop the ball on the green and it would speed though into the rough or worse the tight out-of- bounds a few yards further on.

Chapter 7 – War News

It was a tough winter and backs were truly against the wall in 1941. There was a further call for men to join the Forces and many who had been in reserved occupations such as the police were enlisted. Dad tried again but they still wouldn't take him on in the Navy or as he found out a few weeks later the Army. "Can't have you coughing your guts out in a dormitory of other ranks, Kirkcaldy," said the recruiting officer. The Captain was more sympathetic and as a result dad's duties at work, at the golf club and fire-watching increased and latterly he was responsible for a whole team of elderly gents with poor mobility, hearing and sight who kept the citizens warned of future enemy bombing raids.

Just as the better weather and longer nights came about Dad received devastating news. His closest school pal Davie was killed on 24 May 1941 when HMS Hood was blown up by the Bismarck. Dad later found out a shell had penetrated the aft magazines and the ship sank in less than 5 minutes. Only 3 of the 1,418 crew were rescued and survived. Dad had seen Davie on one occasion when he was home on leave. He enjoyed sailing on the Hood and told Dad he had been trained as an anti-aircraft gunner located towards the stern of the ship and was in a handy position to use his nautical skills to man the ropes when the ship docked or took on supplies from vessels when at sea.

Dad never talked much about Davie's fate preferring to remain with the memory of his ruddy cheeked, cheery fellow fisherman and golf partner. Dad never fished or sailed again as far as I could make out and he had little desire to play golf either unless ordered to accompany the Captain in a foursomes game against some old buffers.

Dad saw Jock a few times but there was usually only time for a drink during his home leave as he had so many friends and relatives to see and a bit of shooting to do on the family estate.

Dad saw more of Brian who was stationed in England for all of his RAF service. He didn't make pilot but his maths skills enabled him to become a navigator, and in time his talents were recognised so as to become a member of 109 Squadron, the first Pathfinder group to fly twin-engined Mosquito bombers. They flew down special radio beams code named Oboe and when the twin beams coincided they dropped incendiary bombs as a guide for the heavy bombers in the rear. They also flew sorties dropping 'Window', great clouds of silver foil to fool the Germans into thinking a large force of bombers was in the air thus diverting German night-fighters towards empty skies and allowing the real bomber force an easier run in on targets.

The wooden Mosquito was an exceptional aircraft ranked along with the Spitfire fighter and Lancaster bomber as the most significant British aircraft of World War 2. Losses among Pathfinder Squadrons were significantly smaller than those among mainstream fighters and bombers. Nevertheless on 30 September 1944 Brian was lost on a raid and now the 1939 golf team was down to 2.

Chapter 8 – Jock Romanes

Jock joined the Royal Scots as an officer and was initially seconded to Intelligence which was fortunate as the 1st Battalion were caught up in Dunkirk and suffered heavy losses with many other men taken prisoner while the 2nd Battalion was based in Hong Kong and succumbed to the Japanese invasion in December 1941. Jock was posted to the reconstituted 2nd Battalion and served in Italy and Palestine with distinction resulting in the award of the Military Medal. In late 1945 he was badly wounded at Monte Gamberaldi, Marradi in North East, Tuscany and eventually evacuated out to a military hospital run by US Forces. There Jock slowly was brought back to health by Mame a nurse from Miami. He had contracted polio but otherwise recovered from his wounds. Dad went to his wedding held in Edinburgh in 1946 with a reception at The Royal Scots Club. Jock then left for America with Mame his bride and went to work for her father who had a large Ford dealership near Palm Springs. Even with a calliper on his leg Jock managed to play golf. Before he left he donated to my father his clubs which Dad had always admired. They had been made by George Nicoll of Leven and were 'Pinsplitter' clubs as endorsed by 3-time Open winner Henry Cotton; 1-4 Woods, 1-9 irons with the putter-being number 9, a 'Howitzer' with a heavy sole like a sand wedge and the 8 iron like a modern wedge.

Jock said once he became settled in the States he was going to play golf again. He was able to use a sit-on buggy and this enabled him to get his handicap down to 4, which was no mean feat - he had been playing off a 2 handicap in 1939.

Jock and his wife came back to Scotland regularly and obviously led a much better life than post War Scots with large cars with automatic transmission and fins, all manner of labour saving household devices and a big ranch-style house with sea views. Jock and Mame had no kids but were devoted to each other. Mum and Dad visited them once before I was born, and a picture of the view from Jock's home had pride of place above his desk in my father's study.

On the 17th of March 1966 Jock and Mame were killed instantly in their Ford Mustang convertible when it was hit amidships at traffic lights by a car being pursued by the police after the occupants had carried out a robbery.

Mum said Dad was devastated after that, as he was now the only survivor of the 38/39 Royal High golf team. She said tried her best to cheer him up and later I realised that must have involved creating me that summer.

I was born on 17 March 1967 so it was no contest what my given name was to be - Mum had her shout when my big sister was born 9 years previously. My birth seemed to inspire Dad despite my long bouts of crying or perhaps that was the catalyst to get out of a nappy-strewn house and hone his game.

My father said he had fitted for the season the last set of 'Kinghorn' tacky leather grips to his bullet-proof Pinsplitters. Dad said the metal was so tough the irons never wore out in 25 years of play. However a week later a large parcel arrived from a firm of Miami lawyers entrusted with winding up the estate of Jock and his wife. It was Jock's new golf clubs just purchased a few months before his death. They were McGregors of the type endorsed by Jack Nicklaus: 1, 3, 4, 5, 6, 7, 8 and 9 irons together with pitching and sand wedges and beautiful persimmon-headed 1, 3 and 4 woods. There was also a flange bladed putter made by George Lowe, the kind used by a lot of American pros. This was an omen and Dad won the Club Championship at Silverfield that year for the 6th time and was pleased to triumph over the young guns and in particular to beat the coming-man Derek Sellar in the final. He won the championship for the next few years and Dad only regained it a further time once Derek had left the club, turned pro and began to play on the fledgling European Tour.

Chapter 9 – Father and Son

Dad had always said he was very happy with my big sister and I could tell she was his favourite, but gradually as I grew up and began asking questions about his disappearances to the golf course, I was taken putting with an elderly uncle with a waxed moustache who had served in the First War. We played the undulating putting green at North Berwick near the Glen links at the east end of the town. Looking back I was rubbish and steered the ball into the holes with numerous touches, but ruling out these frenetic sessions of continuous play I counted my score only by reference to the initial blow of each such bout, plus the final tap in and was pleased to 'win' several holes.

I did however note how old Uncle Harry with the borrowed cleek from the Starter's Hut carefully measured up each putt, and put his club in front of the ball to get a clear line before bringing the club back behind the ball and stroking it sweetly and smoothly off towards the hole. Despite being well into his 70's he beat Dad hands down. I still use that putter pre-stoke drill to this day.

At age 10 I was sent for lessons to the pro, and by 13 was winning the odd hole off my Dad on the rare occasions we played together during my school holidays. I became quite a good Junior and was thrilled one day age 16 to beat Dad, albeit off a handicap of 14 to Dad's 3. The biggest golfing thrill we had was just before I went off to University, we triumphed in the

Father and Son Club Foursomes. He said afterwards it gave him a greater thrill than winning all the Club Championships and in one of our last conversations he put our win up there with his 1939 Royal High team triumph and winning the Club Championship in 1967. When I quizzed him about this choice he did say that my birth had helped him out of a spell of depression after Jock's death. Mum had sent him out of the house and she and my sister looked after me while dad practised and played his way back to health with a determination to win for the friend he admired so much.

He retired the Pinsplitters in 1967 and put them in a glass case in his study. I got a row once for trying them out but I did take them down to Portobello once after Dad's stroke for a quiet 9 holes over the short links and found them nigh on unplayable. Their unforgiving narrow soles cut into the turf when you least expected it, and being blades the ball seemed to go nowhere unless you hit it smack in the middle of the club, when admittedly a strange elasticity kicked in and the ball soared. The trajectory was only let down in terms of distance by the tired elderly fake wood steel shafts. By comparison Dad said the McGregors, once he got the hang of them, were like the difference between a pre-War car with running boards and side valve engine, and a sleek 1960's American car with a V8 motor. The shafts were top class and Dad could hit the 1 iron high off the tee like Jack Nicklaus. He could also drop the ball on the green to a shuddering stop using the wedges which he called his jewels, as they sat nicely behind the ball, and swept cleanly through ball and turf to provide a high steady trajectory.

Chapter 10 – Son Flies the Coop

Shortly after our Father and Son competition triumph I left home to attend Dundee University to study Accountancy. There were lots of subjects I hated at School, but I had an affinity with figures and their logic and perversely enjoyed making both sides of the Balance Sheet add up. I did join the University Golfing Society and had many pleasant outings fuelled with plenty of alcohol to some very prestigious venues although after some of our antics we were not asked back.

I was not good enough to get a Blue and in truth interests in beer, betting on horses and women sadly in that order took over. There were fewer female undergraduates in those days and Accountancy was not a popular course for the female sex. My golf slumped a bit but I did recover somewhat when I came home to start work as a trainee in the accounts section of the North of Scotland Hydro-Electric Board. Once you have left home you should never go back but the pay was modest and Mum and Dad didn't charge much for digs. They did however annoyingly still treat me like a 15 year old complaining about the hours I kept at weekends.

Eventually I moved out and later moved in with Jenny whom I met on the golf course. When that all broke up I went back home for a bit, and was turned off by the whole notion of golf for a year or two as I didn't want to bump into Jenny and her new man. He was a plus 4 handicap boy wonder, who had broken Silverfield's course record by 3 shots with an unbelievable 61 - I could remember when that was a good 9 hole score for me!

Dad was pleased when I settled down a bit and re-joined Silverfield as an adult member. We played a bit together but he was especially pleased to see me win the odd Medal (Handicap Section) and the occasional foursomes title with a variety of partners.

Chapter 11 – The Endgame

I should have seen it coming but I was so busy and full of myself in my thirties. I had been promoted at work was quite popular, though largely unattached. I enjoyed my golf and would like to have been better, but most of the time I didn't put in the hard yards chipping and putting. Occasionally I went home for Sunday lunch and never noticed Dad getting thinner and not playing very much golf. After a particularly fine meal of lentil soup, roast beef, Yorkshire Puddings etc. and Eve's Pudding - sponge and apples with custard, my dad fell asleep in his armchair and I helped Mum tidy up.

"Your Dad's not well you know." "Really?" I replied. "Have you not noticed how much weight he has lost and how he doesn't bother to play golf anymore?" said Mum. "Now that you mention it, yes I suppose so." Well he has got lung cancer probably as a result of his TB, and before that all the fags he smoked as a boy." "Is it bad?" I queried tentatively. "It's probably terminal but they can't give a timescale other than there is not a lot they can do for him." "Why hasn't he told me?" "He didn't want you to worry as he thought you were at last a bit more settled." "Aw Mum, you are always asking about my love life and when there might be grandkids." "That's different! He was working up to tell you but he's not been well these last few days so I thought now was the best time. I'll square it with him later."

A few months later he had a stroke when I had sneaked out for a game of golf one day when I should have been working. The next 18 months were difficult and I moved back to help Mum with dressing, feeding, toileting (a new intransitive verb for me) and changing him. At first it was difficult to make out what Dad was saying as his voice as well as his left side were badly affected. He became frustrated at the effort it took to communicate and how the sounds he produced disappointed him as much as it took us to decipher what he meant.

What made up for all the hard work of being a carer was the quality time we had together watching football and golf on TV and gradually over the months bit by bit I extracted the DNA of Dad's golf from him.

Chapter 12 – Remodelling
the Leith Swing

This vein of conversation started when I innocently asked how dad had blossomed in the 1950s as a golfer and began to win the Club Championship. "Ah well son, as you know as I grew up there was only one golfer for me - Abe Mitchell. But the Leith boys got me playing with a low-flighted linksy swing, but that was useless during the war when all the barbed wire was laid out on the fairways and the Hitler bunker arrived at the 9th. You see, unlike me, Jock had played a lot at Bruntsfield and inland courses like Boat of Garten up near Aviemore which he played when up North shooting - he had a high ball flight which seemed untroubled by the elements. He was taller than me and brought the club right down on the back of the ball every time then took a huge turf and created backspin which sent the ball soaring towards the target. I tried to do that during the War when I played with the Captain but I was a bit hit or miss. After the War however I went to see the Open at St Andrews in 1946 - the won that Sam Snead won, and while he was a wonderful swinger of the golf club I was transfixed by Bobby Locke, the South African who played in immaculate plus fours and a white bunnet. He had a linksy swing and his putting with a simple blade called a Gem was sensational in the way he could move the ball one way or the other when putting, taking a lot of the borrow off the shot. Ultimately fellow pros who played tournaments with him realised they would learn nothing from the line Bobby took with his putts as his ball was usually set off in a right to left draw. I was proved right about him when he won the Open in 1949 and 1950 as well as in 1952 and 1957. I got his book 'Bobby Locke on Golf' when it came out in 1953. I studied it closely and practised hard so that I almost became a clone of the great man's technique. I won the Club Championship 5 times in a row, but I had time on my side and some encouragement at work to take clients out to Silverfield or partner them at outings.

All good things come to an end and the year after my 5th win I had a terrible season. By that time Arnold Palmer had burst on the scene and when we saw clips of him on Newsreels he looked very exciting. I saw him at St Andrews in the Open in 1960 when he finished 2nd but by that time I had already witnessed the next big thing - Jack Nicklaus.

I happened to be down South on business in 1959 and was able to take the day off and go to Sandwich to see the quarter finals of the Amateur Championship. Although a very young and slightly podgy Jack lost 4 and 3 to another American called Hyndman who lost in the final, I was amazed at the height he got on the ball even from a 1 iron off the tee. I wrote enthusiastically to Jock abut Jack and he sent me a copy of 'My 55 ways to Lower your Golf Score' by the great man and it became my new golfing bible. I did love Tony Lema's win at St Andrews in 1964. He was the new guy on the street, the form horse who came over to the UK for the first time with what we now call 'hype' but beat Jack Nicklaus by 5 strokes and was truly majestic. Sadly he died in a plane crash two years later just a few week after Jack won his first Open at Muirfield. After Jock's death earlier in that year I hardly played but was persuaded to go to the last day and Jack was brilliant. I resolved to make further changes to my swing in line with the great man. When I was sent the clubs from Jock's estate, that was the final piece in the jigsaw and gave me new emphasis after a few slump years - you should never give up. I remembered once when I was out once playing a match with Jenny we came across Dad on the practice area in the pouring rain. We had to play that day as it was the last date we could play this tie in the second round of the mixed foursomes so few others were about. "What the hell are you doing, Dad?" I shouted. "Remodelling my swing son" shouted back the octogenarian. It was his way of trying to get the best out of the new ball - the Titleist Pro VI.

Chapter 13 – Last Days

Looking back it was only a matter of time, Mum and I had nursed him for about 18 months which experts will tell you is about the average life expectancy for new arrivals in a geriatric nursing home. When you are involved with a loved one you blind yourself to the obvious and keep looking ahead and suggesting milestones ahead like birthdays and family weddings that provide a path to a continuing future.

One day, a better one for Dad in his inexorable decline, he talked again about his Royal High golf team mates. "Ye see Jock, I've felt guilty all my life ever since I failed that navy medical in 1939. It got worse during the War when I was safe and Davie then Brian were killed and Jock was wounded and crippled. I felt guilty playing golf but if I went out and played, and usually after a slow start, once I got up the hill and looked out on Edinburgh and the Firth of Forth the breeze seemed to blow some of my troubles away. It was like when we did running at school; after a while you got your second wind and all you could do was concentrate on your breathing and putting one foot in front of another. It was the same for me with golf. I concentrated on the round and somehow other distracting and depressing thoughts were temporarily obliterated by the job in hand. Some golfers talk about going into a zone when they get near the ball, size up the shot, select the club and execute their vision with the club. However for me, when I played best I was completely in the zone and thought about the round like a frame of snooker and having to execute each shot to the best of my abilities. I also had to take into account the additional dimensions of the terrain and weather so as to complete the course in the fewest strokes. I played best on my own and had some fantastic scores that no one would believe. However in a game I could chat a bit, but otherwise I was elsewhere and no one could extract me from that with gamesmanship or the like. I knew the optimum way round Silverfield playing to my strengths. In the early days I played the ball low and right to left, but latterly I played high fade and took the hazards on the left side of the course out of play. With a fade the ball didn't run too far on landing so you could focus better on the precise area you wanted the ball to land so as to line up the next shot. Golf courses are laid out generally to get tougher as you try to reach the green. When you mess up a hole you should look back as you walk off the green, not in disgust but in amazement at how easy it is as you look back towards the tee. You can see where each shot should have been played to so as to have a certain putt on the green or perhaps even a single putt opportunity. Nowadays it all seems to be about smashing the ball as far as possible and hacking out with a wedge and lots of brute strength, but occasionally one of the top pros wins on a tricky course with accuracy, skill and guile. It was like a masterclass and I soaked up the words without wondering why he hadn't imparted all this knowledge to me ages ago.

Then Dad went sombre. "On the other hand when I wasn't playing golf, I would get a bit low. I don't know how you all put up with me sometimes especially your Mother. If I couldn't get out to play I like to sit in my study away from you all. " "We noticed that," I interrupted. "Well after I'm gone have a look in the middle shelf of my safe and you will see what I used to ponder over," and he then closed his eyes and dozed off.

I didn't have much time to dwell on that conversation as Mum and I had lot to do to help over the next few weeks - and then he was gone.

Chapter 14 – The Aftermath

On the fateful day when Dad died I had been working late down in the archives at work, out of mobile phone signal range partially to get away from the unending routine of shifts at the office interrupted by panic calls from Mum and spells nursing Dad myself. By the time I got home and saw Dad a few hours after his death his face had crumpled further and it was looking like a different man. His beard had kept growing after death and he wasn't the clean shaven man who had brought me up and been a wonderful role model for me.

The funeral was a blur, the church was packed and I gave the address. We then had a private committal at the crematorium and the wake afterwards. There was a big turn out from Silverfield including all the ancient members who were fit to attend. Old Walter edged up to me, a cup of tea rattling in its saucer in his shaky hand and crumbs from a sausage roll all over his club tie. "Aye yer Dad was a braw man, no much of a War mind, but a great golfer and a modest one tae. Yer no' a patch on him ken, but dinnae let that worry you, be proud, Jock" and at that the old boy turned and wandered off for more savouries and a dram as things had warmed up and whisky was now available as a refreshment.

Once my Mum, sister and I got home we were all totally exhausted, both physically and mentally and went off to bed about 9 o'clock after a cup of tea. That night and in the days afterwards I thought about

Walter's succinct summing up of my Dad's life in a couple of sentences, and my own inadequacies and under achievements both on and off the golf course.

Mum and my Aunt Ruby tidied up the house and we got rid of all the depressing aids to invalid life and aired the downstairs bedroom/sitting room in which Dad had spent his final years. I took all his old clothes to the charity shop, the nappies to an old folks' home and soon the signs of his presence in the house had diminished. I registered Dad's death and we saw the lawyer. He had left nearly everything to Mum as expected, but I was left all his golf stuff and books, and the safe and contents, but my sister got £20,000. My theory about her being the favourite offspring was vindicated. She had stroppy teenage kids and a lazy husband so in a sense Dad was making a final wise and perceptive decision with that bequest.

Mum was tired and at times weepy, and one day called me to say she and Ruby, her sister, were going to Majorca for a week's sun and relaxation away from all reminders of the last 2 years.

I was pleased about that and had started to move back to my flat which I had hardly stayed in during Dad's final illness.

I don't know what it was during that quiet week but one wet day I decided to go back home and take a look at Dad's study and what was left. The sets of clubs which shaped his 70 plus years on the fairway were all there. The Ben Sayers set purchased in single club instalments in the 1930s, the Pinsplitters with the bullet-proof heads which still shone when you wiped the dust off them, and the McGregors which oozed with the quality of latter day Nike VR Pro blades. They were simple with a line across the back dividing the thin top edge from a fatter sole to get the ball up in the air but into a penetrating flight. Dad never really let me touch them. I pulled out his favourite 8 iron where his regular well struck shots had worn the face in and around the sweet spot. I noticed the 5 iron had a piece of lead tape on the sole which had become almost fused to the metal with the passage of time. Dad told me Jock Romanes had put it on and he just kept it there. One day when Dad had new grips fitted by the pro, and the loft and lie of the irons checked, the pro had remarked when Dad had told him how he had acquired the set "Aye well he knew what he was doing as the 5 iron was the only one with an odd swing weight and that tape sorted it out."

Although the clubs looked a bit old fashioned now they felt good in my hands.

I looked at the bookshelf and saw Dad's collection of golf books, in particular the titles by Abe Mitchell, Bobby Locke and Jack Nicklaus. I then noticed on the bottom shelf near his desk among the history books, three volumes which stood out from the others; 'The Sinking of the Bismarck', 'The Pathfinders' and 'The History of the Royal Scots Regiment'. They were for him, no doubt reminders of his three mates.

I rummaged about in the desk drawers; everything was tidy, pens pencils rubbers, a stapler, scissors and a ruler. At the back of the drawer was an old golfer's sweetie tin and inside was what I took to be the safe key. The safe was an old fire-proof model that Dad had bought when his office at work was refurbished. I turned the key a couple of times and despite the fact it had probably not been touched for a bit, the mechanism smoothly clicked and when a big handle was turned the door opened revealing a surprisingly small interior - a Tardis in reverse dwarfed by the strong insulated sides. All Dad's legal papers had been held by the family solicitor for safekeeping and this was a personal hoard of things that were special and personal to my father.

There was a copy of the summer edition of 'Schola Regia', The Royal High School magazine from 1939 showing the victorious Lothian Schools Cup winning team. My father was instantly recognisable on the right standing beside a tall elegant Jock Romanes, the captain with a weather-beaten Davie and a bespectacled Brian on Jock's other side. Each had a hand on the trophy, a modest claret jug. In their other hand, they held a club; Davie and Brian's were woods probably drivers, Jock's was a long iron perhaps a no 3, and Dad held an uncompromising cleek-type blade putter in his hand. I fished about amongst the Ben Sayers set and there it was - 70 years on; a Joe Anderson of Perth 'Special' putter with a hickory shaft and a thin wrap of suede leather for the grip - it looked utterly unplayable!

On the middle shelf was a large manila envelope containing death certificates and war citations for Davie and Brian, a Military Cross citation for Jock, and Distinguished Flying Medal for Brian who had been a sergeant at the time of his death. There were 4 boxes containing various medals. I saw a book entitled 'British Campaign Medal 1914-2005' by Peter Duckers and started to work out what the medals represented and whose box was whose. I correctly guessed Davie's box which contained a green white and blue ribboned Atlantic Star. Davie's mother had received in 1946 after the War and subsequently left it to my father when she died in 1957. Similarly, Brian's box contained the Air Crew Europe Star, The Distinguished Flying Medal and the France and Germany Star for bravery in the invasion of France in 1944 shortly before his death. The biggest box was Jock Romanes' and it held his Military Cross for bravery as an officer, together with all the campaign medals - the Defence Medal, the War Medal, the Africa Star and the Italy Star. In the box was a set of miniatures, copies of these medals which I knew were sometimes worn by veterans with evening dress. The last box was hard to open and was very dusty. It contained a Defence Medal and the War Medal but I had never seen my father wear them. I think he must have felt ashamed to wear them alongside those who had been in the thick of battle and had lost comrades close by. Next to it was a copy of Dad's book of the silhouettes of German planes which he used when on duty as a fire-warden.

It was a small poignant trove of things my father held dear and it felt both a privilege and an intrusion to hold these items personally.

Chapter 15 – Moving On

I dutifully met Mum and Ruby off the Palma plane from their holiday. My mother did look better with a touch of the sun on her face as a contrast to the steely grey Scottish bleak weather she had returned to. "You look awful peely-wally, like you've been in jail all summer." "Thanks Mum. I haven't had time to loaf in the sun." "Time you had a game of golf," said Ruby who had also mellowed in the sun, aided no doubt by a few sherries.

A week or so later there was a brief respite in the weather and one of those crisp sunny late autumn days came along. The sun was weak but with a jersey or two on and little wind, what more did you want to play golf in Scotland? I had been fairly limited in taking foreign trips apart from those through work, and actually hated when the heat got above 20 degrees Centigrade or 70 Fahrenheit. I was a temperate weather creature and anything between 55 and 60 degrees (whatever that was in new money) suited me fine.

I carefully loaded up Dad's McGregor clubs, added the ancient putter and put all the medals in a pocket of the golf bag. A few days before Mum had phoned me to say Dad's ashes were available for collection from the funeral directors. She recalled that he had once said he wanted them scattered on the 9th fairway at Silverfield but wasn't sure if the Committee would allow it. Either way she felt too upset to be present at any such dispersal.

I left it late on in the day as I didn't want to play a full round. As I hoped, the course was quiet and the sun was setting in my face as I teed off, and played due West uphill on Silverfield's daunting start. The irons were remarkably good and needed to be hit with a slightly different swing. A quick wash of the grips before I set off made them feel less worn than they actually were. The putter was truly awful, light, thin, and with a narrow sole that caused me to duff a few putts early on.

However once I got up to the top of the hill and turned back for the 4th to the golden view down towards the Bass Rock and North Berwick Law in the distance, I began to enjoy myself. Six was a good score at some of the holes with these unfamiliar implements, but then on the short par 4 6th I sank a huge putt with the 'Special' for a birdie and the game was on. The 7th and 8th were dispatched in classic par 4s and then I set off up the 9th fairway.

I took my time setting up the ball on a tee as the driver had a small head by modern standards - about 160cc compared to the 460 cc behemoths which greatly facilitate the contemporary game. I put a good swing on the ball and surprised myself when the ball took a low flight and landed softly allowing it to roll up the fairway onto the plateau in pole position. A short shot remained but out-of-bounds was ready at the rear to catch an over eager adrenalin-filled approach shot. Hitler's bunker was no longer the force it was back in the day after its initial excavation. Members complained about its unfairness as they trooped back to play the links after War service and the ladies demanded a special tee which largely kept them away from this hazard, unless their approach shot was a dreadful shank. It was austerity days however - when austerity was a virtue to be borne cheerfully and not a devalued over used political adjective designed to keep the masses oppressed after the suits had stuffed up in 2008.

There were other priorities in getting the course and clubhouse tidied up after years of neglect. Eventually in 1951 when Churchill came back into power as Prime Minister the older members clubbed together in his honour to cut the Hitler bunker down to a more manageable size. Soil had to be brought in as it seemed a lot of the original earth had evaporated when the bomb exploded. Scores improved as a result, and the 9th hole hoodoo which had led to many a promising card being torn up before embarking on the second 9 was a thing of the past. Unless that is you let the perverse golfer situated between your ears lead you to believe you still needed a superhuman shot to reach the 9th green and let it roll gently up to the flag, and not out-of-bounds. The most obvious beneficiary of this new regime was a certain Mr R "Bob" Kirkcaldy who was able to play his Leith Links-Abe Mitchell-Bobby Locke golf to perfection and run up a string of championship victories.

There was no one around so gingerly I took the plastic bag out of the golf bag and looked at the grey granules inside which had once been my Dad. He played straight and was rarely in trouble through to the green, so I slowly walked around in circles on the fairway scattering the ashes discretely. Some of the dust was taken away in a gust which appeared eerily as if on cue. Once I was finished I put the bag away and selected the 8 iron for a pitch and run. I struck the ball sweetly and it landed softly short of the green and ran on leaving a tempting side-hill putt of about 8 feet for glory. I felt a bit shaky holding the simple blade over the ball then I remembered Uncle Harry's tip and lined the face up with the intended line of travel then placed the club behind the ball, exhaled and concentrated on a smooth stroke. The ball arced its way down from the high right side but I seemed to have misread the putt and it began to die and rolled towards the low side of the hole. The ball stopped then fell in backwards and slightly uphill into the hole as if it was defying gravity. The golfing Gods were with me.

I turned to survey the scene, I was in the zone and darkening clouds and spots of rain did not deter me. I fished the dusty box out of my golf bag and pinned my Dad's medals on my jersey. I was going to go on to the 10th tee, continue into the twilight and post a score!

My Golfing Romance

Chapter 1 – A Useful Partner

Not that I am a great feminist or anything but I was pleased to join a mixed golf club when I was accepted for Silverfield. It had been a mixed club since its inception over 100 years ago, and although for many years the ladies had enjoyed lower fees in return for restrictions on when they might play, the age of equality had forced changes. The membership worked through these without the angst of the R&A, Muirfield and the like who just looked plain silly. It never ceased to wonder how such an elderly out-of-touch body like the R & A had such power over the game, yet wondered why it had ceased to so popular and how fewer people played this wonderful game.

Mind you as a younger man I thought if I entered the mixed foursomes each year I might end up with an attractive partner drawn from the hat, but the reality was that for about ten years my random partners were drawn from the mature segment of the ladies' section, and when they turned up on a squally evening wearing thick specs I knew we were doomed, despite their high handicaps. This was the whole ethos of the club mixed foursomes; you couldn't chose your partner as you could in the men-only equivalent, and it was not the done thing to practise with your lady partner between rounds.

One year however I was drawn to play with Ms Jenny Hinton, who played off 10 compared to my 14 handicap

JENNY HINTON

at the time. I was intrigued and checked up on her in the Members' book. She was a new member and stayed in a flat in an expensive suburb of Edinburgh.

She sounded confident on the phone when we were arranging our tie and looked the real deal when she turned up 10 minutes before our tee off time on the night. She was about 5 ft. 7" auburn hair, of medium build, clearly sporty and smartly but fashionably dressed in a matching green outfit of a skirt and top and pushing an electric trolley filled with new, shiny, top-of-the-range Taylor Made clubs.

"You must be Jock", she said. "Did you have a description to go on?" I replied. "Oh yes. You drive a classic car and could do with a good tidy up, I was told by old Mrs Simpson."

I rolled my eyes then looked down at my unpolished shoes, crumpled trousers and jersey with an acid burn on it which had occurred when I had to replace the car battery.

"Hopefully my golf isn't too shabby," I replied as best I could to try and save face from the brusque opening gambit.

The convention was that the men teed off at the first and the ladies walked up the hill a fair distance ready to play the next shots in classic foursomes alternative shots mode. It was a format designed by elderly men in fancy golf clubs to maximise time back at the bar and make the most of their dwindling skills. It was a great leveller too; you were only as good as the combination of your best shots and those of your partner. I had however seen some of the older Members go round in under 2 hours despite walking slowly but they played steadily and safely and never spent much time looking for a lost ball. My tee shot was a dreadful swipe and scuttled about 60 yards along the ground, which left my partner with a 100 yard walk back to play her shot-Bad Start!

Despite Jenny playing a stylish recovery we lost the first hole and after I missed a putt at the next we were soon 2 down then 3 down when I lost a ball off the tee.

I could see the other couple were chatting away whereas a dampener of silence fell over our partnership.

Jenny's tee shot at the 4th was OK but not her best and it was me to play next.

It was 140 out, downwind and you could not be long at this green as bunkers lurked behind as well as each side. I kept my head down, had a few steady practice swings and launched a smooth stroke where the club skimmed the turf as I prefer. The ball soared over the flag struck a bank at the rear and rolled back into the hole for an unlikely eagle which won us the hole. Jenny beamed and gave me a hug when I caught up with her. "I had heard that you had your moments, but I was getting worried when I saw few signs of life," she exclaimed, in what I was to find later was her straightforward, no-nonsense style.

Slowly we fought back. On our good holes we gelled and won and when there was the odd bad shot we managed to half a few.

By the turn we were level and had the match won on the 16th green -3 up with 2 to play. It was just as well, as the weather began to close and the four of us trouped in and had a drink. I posted up our names as winners on the competition notice board then put my clubs in the locker and set off for the car park. When I got there I found Jenny trying to start her new Ford Focus company car. I offered to help out, but of course being a modern vehicle with sophisticated electronics throughout, there not much I could do other than to check there was fuel in the tank. "I knew you'd do that," said Jenny. "Well if you'd called the AA they would asked the same thing."

"I can't wait for them at this time of night!" wailed Jenny; "I have meetings first thing". "Don't worry, I can drive you home in my old analogue motor." So I squeezed Jenny's stuff into the back of my MGB GT and, despite a few misfires and a slipping clutch, got her home.

"I'll see you in the next round then," I said. "I'll look forward to that, Mr Kirkcaldy!" Jenny replied with mock formality and she was gone after putting her stuff in her garage then closing the electric door behind her and walking through the back into her smart flat.

Chapter 2 – My Game gets better

Our next tie was two weeks later and somehow I felt myself getting all excited about it. I went up 3 nights in a row to the Club to practise in the nets and to chip and putt. I surprised myself by getting some new trousers, a shirt and slipover. "My! Is that you, Jock? You do brush up well!" said Jenny coming out of the pro's shop in a silky two-piece skirt and top outfit, as I walked up to the first tee.

Our opponents were a dangerous combo of a former Club champion 'Wee' Davie Sim (because he was 6 ft. 7") who still played off 3, coupled with an older lady, Doris de Gaudin who was off 15 but had long experience at the Club and had been a low handicapper in her prime. We started off better this time but somehow we found ourselves 2 down at the turn. I felt I was playing out of my skin and Jenny was solid as usual. Eventually a breakthrough came at the 13th where we won 3 holes in a row which put us in the lead. I hit some great drives which ended up on the fairway and holed a few vital putts to maintain our narrow lead to the 18th.

"See and do well," said Wee Davie as we walked towards the Club House after halving the last to win the tie. "We fancied ourselves to reach the Final so don't let us down!"

There was an agonising gap over the summer months until our next tie came up. In the interim I had my clubs re-gripped by the Club pro and played and practised regularly. I studiously avoided playing in the Monthly Medals lest my handy handicap was trimmed to a more realistic figure commensurate with my improving skills. I comforted myself that the keen members were all at it. Some of the male duos played in foursomes' tournaments in Ireland in the summer and even won prizes but somehow the cards they put in to win the prizes never filtered back to the Club and the Handicap Secretary.

I couldn't possibly suggest our next opponents fell into that category but Fred McMenemy and Siobhan Drogheda seemed to know each other well, and of course with names like that came from Ireland. They gelled from the start and while we didn't play badly, we only won the odd hole and halved a few and by the turn were 3 down.

There was a delay ahead of us and we took the time to have a frank team talk. "You need to find the fairway off the tee and sink a few of those makeable putts I am setting up for you!" hissed Jenny. "Aye well stop going out- of- bounds like you did at the 9th after my brilliant tee shot!" I snapped back.

"OK, OK what's our plan to be to get out of this spot"? Jenny always knew the right thing to say in crucial moments though I suspected some of these gems must come from Management School. "Well Captain, it's you to tee off at the 11th so where do you want my second shot to land after your fine tee shot?" I said, deploying the straight-but-sarcastic gambit Jenny seemed to use all the time when she spoke to me.

"Thank you, Corporal Kirkcaldy, the green would be fine but if not try not to miss on the low side. I don't mind if it is a bit short and I can chip the ball on the green and see it run up to the flag."

That request was easier said than done. Jenny's tee shot was a good one and longer than her opponent's but left me with that tantalising distance from the green that I knew I hit only once or twice a season. Leaving the ball a bit short and left on the high side of the fairway is a bit difficult for a slicer like me where my left to right ball flight was going to be accentuated on landing by the slope of the close cropped fairway. My ball was going to roll down the hill and probably stop blocked behind the holly tree where I ended up as often as not. I had thought about the shot as soon as we had crested the hill and Jenny's ball came into view. By the time I was beside the ball and had checked how it was lying I had made up my mind; in the amateur game at my level there is no time for long thinks; people would regard you as being indecisive. On the other hand I have rushed so many shots in my impatience, so maybe the pros have got it right (apart from the really slow boring ones). Jenny had caught up and was at my side and I could sense was about to 'make a suggestion'. I put my finger to my mouth to silence the thought and pulled out my 4 iron. It was the only club I could hit a right-to-left draw, after honing my skills on the idiosyncratic 16th tee with its wicked 90 degree bend 150 yards down the fairway. I had to allow for the ball lying below the level of my feet which naturally causes the ball to fly right. I lined the shot up for the left of the green and then adjusted my feet to swing the club flatter and round my body.

Out of the corner of my eye I noticed Fred's shot had flown promisingly towards the green but the combination of hitting a slight fade and the slope sent the ball scuttling past the green on the low side where it ended up 30 yards downhill, not in holly bush country but not ideal.

I made good contact and the ball sped low under the breeze and swung to the left landing softly in the semi-rough about 10 yards short of the green. "I'll take that!"

snapped Jenny and sped off towards the ball. By the time I'd got there Siobhan had seen her ball miss the green and roll back down the slope near to her feet and Jenny had chipped to 3 feet. Fred's shot, their fourth, landed on the green but was a long way from the flag, and despite a brave effort by Siobhan to put pressure on me her ball slipped past the cup and the hole was conceded. We were now only 2 down.

It was a turning point in the match but more so was the rain which came down in a deluge as we played the next hole. There were ties being played to a finish behind us so we couldn't shelter for long. After agreeing to half the twelfth, we then won all remaining holes and shook hands on the 17th green which looked on the scoreboard to have been a comfortable win - 3 up with 1 to play.

We were all soaked as we trudged in. No one felt the urge to play home along the tricky 18th and hot showers were all we had on our minds. Our opponents scuttled away - Jenny winked mischievously and suggested that they might be having an affair. "They might just have time for a quickie before they go home to their respective suburban lives. How's your love life, Jock?" smiled Jenny. "Not as good as my golf." I replied as wittily as I could while trying to conceal years of abject failure. "You could always invite me for a drink and tell me all about it."

Jenny had arrived by taxi so once again joined me in my MGB and we set off to the Bridge Inn pub on the Forth and Clyde Canal. I started with a coke, but Jenny had a couple of glasses of dry white wine and after an hour or so it seemed natural for us to have dinner together. Jenny persuaded me to share a bottle of wine over dinner and before I knew where we were she had booked us into a room for the night before I could order a taxi home.

"Don't play too much golf. Two rounds a day are plenty." - Harry Vardon

By the next round we were an item and coasted to an easy two hole success over our opponents whose golf and chat were so dull I forget the details of that match. By semi-final time, I had moved into Jenny's smart flat and all seemed to be going swimmingly. Perhaps love had banished all negative swing thoughts made me play with a more relaxed rhythm, at one with the club and at peace with the world rather than simply using it to thrash the ball. Doughty but middle aged opponents were duly dispatched on the 18th green after a close and thrilling match during which I felt supremely confident. It wasn't just me of course, as Jenny and I gelled, playing to each other's strengths and avoiding our weaknesses, so I was never left with a shot on the course that put me under huge pressure.

One day in a quiet spell at work I thought about Jenny and the past few months; I couldn't believe my luck and the final seemed like it would be a dawdle.

Chapter 3 – The game bites back

However a few weeks can be a long time in golf - longer and more problematic than politics. Our conversations had been turned subtly by Jenny to buying new curtains and carpets, asking when I was going to sell my flat and what did I think of becoming a father. I tried to take this all in my stride, but rapidly I was getting out of my comfort zone just as I used to tease the lads when one got hitched and gradually ceased to participate in our day-long outings. Subsequently they could occasionally be seen driving back from IKEA with furniture strapped to the roof of the car, or more radically pushing a pram, or even horror of horrors, a double-buggy. Gerry, an old mate from school, even ended up with triplets and disappeared from sight for about 20 years.

I don't really want to talk about that final. The Hon John McDermid, the posh chairman of a huge engineering company and future Club Captain was a dour but pleasant opponent and Clara Nixon, who seemed to move in the same circles as John was the reigning woman's Club Champion. Although we got 8 stokes' handicap giving us an extra shot at most of the difficult holes on the course we were soon 4 down despite a breezy start winning the first and halving the second.

Neither of us played anywhere near our best and each of us found ourselves left with impossible shots which is no recipe for success in foursomes. We started snapping at each other and I was almost glad when we shook hands on the 13th green after being whacked 7 and 5. The Hon John was very gracious and Clara chatted away with Jenny complimenting her on her salmon pink outfit which even I knew is usually a disarming line of conversation. We agreed to walk back to the Club House cutting an exaggerated sweep from the far end of the course across several fairways and quickly down the 18th. We had a quick drink with our victors then I drove us home in silence. Back home, it didn't take long to have a huge row about nothing. I said some injudicious things when my golf was blamed for our downfall. I accepted this criticism with alacrity and blamed my poor form on all the pressure recently poured over me with paint shade cards, curtain samples, sofa offers and worst of all, baby talk. I couldn't imagine a Ryder Cup captain exhorting a performance from his team with such a diet of dilemmas, dreariness and hypothetical responsibility.

"I thought you had grown up, Jock and stopped being a schoolboy. However it's clear you don't have the balls to be a man and make some commitments. Time will soon run out for me and at this rate your time will never come!"

That was enough. I felt a rage as the sword of truth cut me in half. I walked out of the room and slammed the door. I grabbed a few things-daft stuff, like my shelf of golf books and a toy model MGB as well as some shaving stuff and stormed out of the house and into my car. At the first set of traffic lights I switched off my mobile phone and pulled out the battery.

Chapter 4 – The Long Sulk

I grabbed a fish supper on the way home - always a comfort in troubled times - like when I used to stagger home alone from another unsuccessful night at the Students' Union dance. I didn't put the house lights on. I had no curtains to pull in my flat - waste of money and I watched wallpaper TV all night until I fell asleep in my chair.

My flounce continued at work and I told the switchboard telephonist not to put any calls through to me from a certain Ms Jenny Hinton. A few days later I was told by the receptionist an attractive, but slightly tearful young woman had left four black plastic bags in the foyer saying they were my worldly goods.

Eventually after a few weeks I put my mobile phone back together and saw four messages had been left. I played them through once then deleted them immediately. Looking back a year or two later when at a low ebb I could still recollect their content and tone. The first one was conciliatory but without any apology, the second pleaded for a response, the third contained an ultimatum and the fourth indicated an intention to drop off my things; she would have liked to deal with them more radically but she wasn't going to waste energy on a timewaster.

I played a few games of golf at times I knew I would not bump into Jenny, but word of our split had gone ballistic round the Club and news of my flounce-out had made me a laughing stock. I put away the clubs for the season which turned into a year and started drinking a bit too much and feeling sorry for myself. I tried to justify my actions as Jenny had seemed to be far too controlling for a laid back gent like myself.

I lost myself in my job to some extent and found more of my friends had succumbed to relationships and only the drunks, bores and the undateable were left in my social milieu, and I fitted all of those categories.

I didn't see Jenny for several years as I heard she was going out with Peter McHarg, a tall good-looking (I hate to admit) Challenge Tour golfer who held the Silverfield course record. He was also an accountant with a degree from Stirling University in Sports Management. He had intended joining a management company but after a stellar amateur career turned pro "for a laugh for a few years first" but seemed talented enough to make the European Tour. His Dad was loaded too, so he had plenty of options. I instinctively hated him although I had never met him, but had merely seen him from afar and had no desire to meet him on a number of counts, one of which was in case I punched him. Now why would a thought like that creep into my otherwise peace-loving existence?

I tried to blank Jenny out of my mind but was intrigued a couple of years after our split to hear that she was pregnant but the couple had not yet married. I had resumed playing at the Club and never saw Jenny, no doubt she had other more important things to do. I disciplined myself not to check the Members' Register either to check if she was still a member or what her current address was - she was just part of my uneven past.

Chapter 5 – The New Man

Five years passed and I had inherited Ruaridh Morrison's house and his 1930's clothes, car and golf clubs and immersed myself in the Duke's (as we used to call him) lifestyle. I had always admired the Duke's style and was shocked to find out after he had died without any relatives that had left his entire estate to me - his latter-day golf partner. His estate included his pagoda-roofed, suburban art deco detached bungalow, complete with period fittings and furnishings, a classic 1930s Squire 2+2 seater sports car and an ancient set of pre-World War II golf clubs.

I sold my flat and used the money to freshen the Duke's house but mostly to get the old car fettled.

It took a while to get used to playing with 80 year-old E R Whitcombe bladed irons and wooden woods of a similar vintage, but I watched the players at the hickory championships, and while my ones had period-correct steel shafts, I changed my swing a bit to cope with the weaker shafts. It took me about 15 months, but in the June medal I teed off early on at 8 30 and made the most of the vestiges of the dew on the greens, and putted firmly and true with an uncompromising cleek of a putter improbably called a 'Gem' shooting a 79 for a net 65.

I had a brief drink and checked on the early returns before roaring home in the Squire.

I parked the car, collected my faithful Westie terrier call Tam (now my only true friend) and walked down the road in my golfing tweeds for a pint of milk and some rolls, when a blonde woman with two children shouted across the street "Is that you Jock?"

I turned and looked and was about to walk on when I sensed something familiar, the height, shape, voice, manner, and under the blonde locks the face of a slightly older but wiser Jenny. I ran over and we looked at each other then instinctively hugged. The children, two girls, chorused in unison - "Who is that funny man, Mummy?"

"What happened to your lovely brunette hair?" I exclaimed impulsively but stupidly. "That wasn't natural either. Did you not notice, Jock?" she smiled. "Err, I think I was busy looking at the rest of you" I replied clumsily. Jenny laughed and the old twinkle was back in her eyes. Her daughters were fascinated with Tam the dog, who for once was in a good mood and enjoying being petted. "Have you time for a coffee?" I found myself blurting out. "That would be fun!" said Jenny."

We went to a nearby dog-friendly cafe for a coffee, and caught up on lost time, in between looking after the twins, Isla and Flora. At one point we put them on a Thomas the Tank engine ride in the foyer, and had a more adult conversation. I told Jenny I had been an idiot and was now a walking museum piece having inherited an elderly member's lifestyle; she laughed just like she used to do. "Did it come with curtains and carpets?" she twinkled at me.

"How are you and wonder boy doing then?" I inquired looking at the two happy girls who by now were busy tying a pink ribbon on the head of an amazingly compliant Tam.

"Oh that crashed and burned six months after the girls were born. He cheated on me when he was away on Tour, and when I found evidence of his philandering one weekend when he came home after missing the cut at the Russian Open, we had a row, following which he punched me in the face and broke my jaw".

"I called the police immediately, even before an ambulance, and he was taken away and prosecuted, but acquitted thanks to his Daddy hiring a top QC to humiliate me in court and get him off with a silky submission to the sheriff. I got civil lawyers on the job and took steps to prevent him seeing the girls. I was advised to let him have some contact but he hasn't seen them since last Christmas. He blew up on Tour and now works for a Sports Betting company setting the odds for punters betting on golf tournaments. Can you imagine such a daft way to make a living, Jock?" "It sounds OK, I bet he makes a packet." "I am sure he does but I think he bets and loses a lot of it and wastes the rest on office girls." I was taken aback by this torrent of information and after a pause asked the only lame question I could summon up. "So what do you do now?" I inquired. "I work 3 days a week, as money from that idiot for the kids comes erratically and I am living with my parents who moved up to Edinburgh to give me some baby-sitting cover." "Once you've left home you should never go back," I retorted from harsh personal experience. "Don't I know!" replied Jenny with an exasperated tone. "They're very sweet but it's driving me mad. I feel guilty about going out with my girlfriends for an occasional night out."

Flora nearly fell out of the novelty train but Jock neatly caught her in time and so the quintet headed off out of the shopping centre, then dawdled in the same general direction when Isla announced she needed the toilet, big time. They were near Jock's house so he directed the group there. Afterwards Jenny, amazed at what she saw, asked for a tour of the house and took in the floral curtains and carpets, art deco furniture, Belfast sink, larder and ancient gas cooker on stilts.

Chapter 6 – Pre-Nuptials

"It's all very tidy, Jock but it's a bit of a museum piece" was her final analysis. "I know, but I'm unsure how to improve and restore it sympathetically. I have never developed any skills in that area", I said with a wry smile which nodded back to my previous stupidity. "Mummy, this is a brilliant house and there is a lovely garden that Tam has shown us!" said Isla. "It's much nicer than Granny and Grandpa's flat!" echoed Flora. "Well you must come again" I replied expansively with new confidence. "We love your little car, yes we do" chorused the girls.

Despite some initial misgivings, I persuaded Jenny to sit in the front of the car and the girls squeezed in the back. There were no seatbelts but I promised to drive slowly and soon we arrived at the grandparents' flat.

"When can we see wee Tam, yes when?" said the girls. "Soon" I replied emphatically. "Your Mummy and I will fix up a trip. Tam loves the seaside and the chance to get a bit of ice cream." "Well that's settled" replied Jenny in a neutral fashion. "Did you ever start using a mobile phone again?" "Yes" I replied sheepishly and removed an elderly small Motorola phone of the folding variety. Jenny winced but rapidly entered my number in her contacts. "Give **me** a ring sometime." she said with her old assertiveness.

Six months later we were married. It seemed a bit of a whirlwind but we took things cautiously to begin with so that the girls would not be hurt if it all fizzled out.

We had some great days out and Jenny brought a girlfriend over who was an interior designer and came up with some good ideas to retain the art deco heritage of the house but adapt it into a modern family home. I was smitten again by Ms Jenny Hinton and one spring day when the five of us were walking on the esplanade to Cramond, girls on their scooters and a roving Tam on his lead I popped the question.

"I thought you'd never ask" said Jenny in her usual sarcastic but warm way. "Well what do you say?" I replied. I want to be with you and help bring up the girls if I may." "You'd be good at that. I think I need a pre-nuptial contract however," said Jenny sounding ominous. "Anything you want, as long as Tam is part of the family." I said hopelessly. "I shall be happy to marry you Jock. You have improved a lot since the last time but one thing I do not want to risk is that we must never play competitive golf together. I would like to get back to playing, and I think we can interest the girls, but I do not want to go through that roller coaster of emotions on the links with you again. We always seemed to be behind in the games we won and briefly ahead in the one we lost disastrously!" "That will be no problem," I replied. "With golf clubs like mine no one wants to be my partner in a foursome!"

Was it an Ace?

Chapter 1 – The Perfect Shot

What keeps you going as a duffer is that one good shot. It may be the only one of the round, but it keeps you going until the next time. By contrast, professionals being debriefed by the journalists after a sub-par round seem to be able to drone out details of every shot made. I try to forget most of them afterwards.

The ideal shot to remember would of course be a hole in one. Kids of 7 have done it and guys in their 90s hitting a driver at a short par 3 have pulled off the feat. I am getting to the stage that I would take a hole in one however pathetic the shot may have been.

"Drive for show, and putt for dough." - Eric Brown

So every time I crest the summit at the blind 10th at Silverfield and the green is empty I invariably check the hole before spending the next 10 minutes trying to find my ball.

What drives me must involve the same DNA as old Budgie at the club who pours a small fortune into the one armed bandit most weekends, but as far as I know has yet to experience the noise of coins pouring out in a jackpot pay-out – that much advertised promise on the side of the machine.

Looking back over 50 years of indifferent golf I can reel off most of the truly great (by my standards) shots I have played. At the long downhill par 4 ninth back in the day, I duffed a drive whereby the ball did not clear the teeing area. My next shot was at least roughly level with where my drive should have been. I then struck a superb 4 wood downhill about 270 yards leaving the ball 12 inches from the flag for a tap in par. There must have been a tailwind- it was the summer, as I have never come within 50 yards of emulating this feat.

I can remember too as a young teenager at Goswick near Berwick-upon-Tweed striking a lady's 5 iron I had, 120 yards on to the green and sinking the resultant 35 feet putt.

So each round I go out and start to play rubbish, but fear not, a short hole is coming up which is at least in range of my driver and sometimes even in reach with an iron. Who knows, I could end up breaking 100 with 4 aces, 13 7s and a par 4 at the 18th!

Chapter 2 – The Near Misses

When I think of how few twos I have had, it gives me a further clue about my lack of success at acing any hole.

Silverfield's course layout didn't help too much either. The second was a short part 3 to a plateau green which I rarely reached due to it being too early in the round, and I was not yet in the groove. Maybe the short pseudo macho practice swings on the first tee were not sufficient to make each shot in the round count, but then a round of golf takes so long I could never be bothered wasting time by turning up early and doing the full warm up before playing.

New equipment - clubs, balls and the like don't seem to make much difference. The extra length on a short hole is neither here nor there; accuracy is most important, what the manufacturers call minimum shot dispersal. I wish I had kept that cheap 7 wood with the metal shaft and smallish head. It was the only club I could play with a bit of draw. It was handy at the 7th where I almost holed out once when the flag was right at the back of the long green. I remembered it could be a bit soggy there, and I heaved this wood all I could and the ball soared with a light right to left bend away from the out of bounds to land softly near to the hole to the wonderment of my playing companions. I think I converted the short putt for a 2, but was so euphoric about that shot I can't honestly remember. What I do know is that I never repeated the feat. Balls went out-of-bounds and on one occasion my swing was so quick on the backswing that my partners advised it was less than two feet. I duffed the ground behind the ball, and it didn't go much further either. What was even more embarrassing was it happened in the club foursomes, and my partner had to walk back from his hopeful vantage point near the green to try and execute a wonder shot from rough near to the tee. Needless to say he did not and our challenge fizzled out shortly thereafter. I then gave the 7 wood to a friend along with the so called matching 1, 3 and 5 woods. In truth the driver was rubbish, the 3 wood was difficult but the 5 was a gem and the 7 worked brilliantly, at least once as I have described. I miss it and have to resort to trying to bump a 5 iron on to the green and hope it threads through the 2 guarding bunkers, while most people play a 7 iron over it all and let it run a bit towards the hole from the front end of the green.

Chapter 3 – The Might Have Beens

I won't bore you with more 'might have beens'. About 25 years ago when the children were small, my wife had a friend with children about the same age, and a husband who was a keen golfer. The wives were keen to have a girls' natter while the children played, so Munro Sutherland organised a game for us at Mortonhall, a keen players' club set up on the hills on the South side of Edinburgh, next to the legendary Braid Hills course. The fact that Munro played off 7 and I was a duffer did not seem to put him off, as I was his legitimate excuse to get out of the house and avoid witnessing children having tantrums and /or being sick.

It was fairly early in the year, and we knew there would only be time for about 9 holes before we would be posted missing, as doubtless by that time the kids would be restless and continually interrupting the mothers' chat.

We played about 4 or 5 holes out and then began to get stuck behind a group of four players. Munro suggested we cut in neatly before another fourball trundling down the 13th. This we did-bending the rules and etiquette of golf slightly by cutting in half way down the empty 14th fairway.

"Let's play it as a par 3" suggested Munro, and quickly teed up a ball about 150-160yards out. He hit his usual steady shot honed in early years over the links of Dornoch where he grew up.

I selected my favourite 6 iron and hit a decent shot which seemed to go fairly straight before it dipped over the rise and disappeared from sight. We walked up and Munro quickly found his ball just short of the green and pitched up dead with a 9 iron before we set out to look for my ball.

"Yours was a stronger shot that mine, so it's probably in the rough at the back of the green" said Munro helpfully.

I took out my pitching wedge and set about scouring the damp rough when Munro who was behind me shouted "It's in the hole!" I couldn't believe it as the build up had all been so normal. Sure enough I recognised my slightly scruffy ball nestling in the hole and retrieved it gently. I was so shocked I never even kept that ball.

We were a bit late back to the tea party but any rebukes that there might have been were swiftly forgotten and I may have had an extra piece of cake by way of celebration.

On reflection it had been a good shot, but I had not had the satisfaction of seeing it drop in the hole. For all I know some kind animal knocked it in out of pity for me missing again. In addition I was a young family man with years of golf ahead of me and lots more opportunity to play as the girls grew up and needed less attention.

Sadly that was not to be. My years at Silverfield have honed the modest golfing skills I possess, and despite playing more often, scoring better and becoming more consistent, I have never had a proper ace. That 6 iron cut in shot all these years ago will just have to do. I leave it to you readers to act as jury and decide whether it was a hole in one, or just a quick pragmatic shot in a bounce game to help us get home in a respectable time for a children's tea party.

How to Cure your Slice for £2.49

Chapter 1 – The Curse of the Slice

It's amazing to think back how long I have played golf without scaling the heights, and reeling off 19 majors to pip Jack Nicklaus's record and give Tiger Wood a new target to tackle. On the other hand it's not surprising when one's golf has been sporadic, interrupted by full-time work and family duties, plus the occasional laziness when I have looked out the window at the cold, wet, gusty weather and gone back to bed. I did so in the sure and certain knowledge that my swing would never cope with the conditions, and my dreaded slice would see the ball soar into the sky then descend in a destructive left to right parabola into thick rough where the ball's resultant resting place often turned out to be too elusive to discover. The old adage is 'never take a golf tip from a duffer' to which in recent years might be added 'see a PGA professional instead and sign up for a programme of video- enhanced lessons!'

"If you think it's hard to meet new people, try picking up the wrong golf ball." - Jack Lemmon

When I think back after three seasons of lessons as a boy I was quite good for my age as a teenager but didn't play so much - in horse racing terms I was a promising two year old, but didn't train on to be a successful classic three year old. Worse still, when the dreaded slice haunted my golf in my early twenties, by which time I was playing with older guys from work, one of them told me to shorten my long languid swing- he was a duffer of course and since then I have been blessed with a short quick swing with no pause at the top. I like to think I was influenced by the brisk tempo of multiple Open Golf Champion Tom Watson.

So I toiled on playing golf intermittently as the job became more intense and the family grew. Early metal woods gave me an extra 12-15 yards as promised but it was all slice and eventually they were retired. I teed off with a one iron for several years, finding that a loss of distance with more certainty of landing on the fairway or at least not in deep rough was much more conducive to better scoring golf.

For one reason or another I never had any more golf lessons for about 25 years when I went to a night school for a winter season, hitting practice balls in a school gym with an eight iron off a mat. This helped my confidence a bit especially as most of the rest of the class were beginners or even worse duffers than me, but did little to cure the slice.

Once I joined a club again in my forties, I got a few lessons from the pro, and what with reading copious golf books, watching the US PGA golf tour on TV, and of course the advent of much better golf equipment and balls, my slice on a good day is what I am pleased to call a power fade. This is a predictable left to right shot which tends to stay in play if you set yourself up aiming for the left rough and trusting the ball to turn into the fairway.

Chapter 2 – Industrial Injury

With a massive titanium headed driver, a decent ball perched on a high tee even I never miss and rarely hit a complete duff. Problems come thereafter with long approach shots; despite lining up carefully and trying to keep my body and swing in line with my target, slightly to the left of where I think the ball will end up, slices continue to be the norm.

One evening after my partner had cooked a fine meal of steak and all the trimmings she indicated a wish to have some chocolate ice cream and I readily agreed to get her some from the fridge. The tub had been opened before and the contents looked a bit frosty. I gathered a bowl and the scoop and started to extract some of the contents. This proved difficult and I strained away with the blunt scoop. I even changed hands and held the tub in my right hand to gain a better hold and twisted the scoop with my left. I felt something give in my left elbow which wasn't painful. However all of this eventually led me to using a knife. Subsequently I felt my elbow was sore, not excessively so, but I lost a bit of strength and found it difficult to lift heavy things above my chest. It was a nagging pain and although I could play golf I felt sore afterwards. I must have tweaked a tendon, and given I had reached an elderly fifty, it was taking an age to sort itself out.

One day as I was driving along the road I saw a chemist's sign. Having brooded about the problem elbow over the preceding months, I stopped the car went in and bought a Tube-A-Grip elastic elbow bandage for £2.49 (other brands of athletic or geriatric bandages are available). I was told not to use it too often or too long so I stuck it in my golf bag and put it on next time when I went out for a game. The results were dramatic; the bandage not only prevented my elbow from getting sore, but also kept my left arm straight and eliminated the slice. The power fade almost disappeared too! I even tried an elastic bandage on the right arm, but felt that might be against the spirit of golf. Around that time I bought a cheap Russian-made self-winding watch. Despite being right handed I have always worn a watch on my right hand as I found it easier to put on. I have always worn a watch while playing golf as I have usually had to watch my time, and if I remembered to wear a golf glove always kept it on the entire round even when putting. I began to notice that while wearing the big watch, my shots had a tendency to draw and fly from right to left (a draw), which often gives a lower more penetrating flight with a fair run on landing. My experiments on this front ended when said watch broke down shortly after going out of guarantee, and I found it would cost more than it was worth to fix.

Chapter 3 – Trying to Spread the Work

My elbow got better, and the fraying and yellowing bandage still rests in a crumpled box in the bottom of a pocket in my golf bag. I often ponder what would have been if I kept wearing it. I sent an e mail in to golf magazine about this inexpensive way of curing the golfer's biggest curse but astonishingly it was never published; after all they have a magazine to produce each month with more expensive solutions to advertise like sets of ghastly distended anti-slice woods and irons with bent necks. These clubs look as though someone discovered the anti-slice solution after hitting the ground with the club after a bad shot, and finding the damaged remains played more to their liking.

A few years ago when The Open Championship was taking place at Muirfield, I went along to a practice day which was very enjoyable especially as the crowds were smaller, the players more relaxed - even smiling occasionally, and there was room to stroll through the tented village and other stalls.

A group of PGA pros were offering free ten minute lessons. None of us duffers were interested in learning to putt better and there was only a short queue to the section dealing with the golf swing. What's your problem sir, a cheery pro from Sheffield asked? "50 years of shit golf" I replied, "oh and I'm having a bit of trouble with my one iron" I added for good measure. "We don't do one irons now the pro replied; they were generally regarded as difficult to play. Most sets of irons nowadays start with a five and you use hybrid clubs, a cross between a wood and an iron from 250 to about 170 yards to the hole. We've only got a short time here what's your main fault?" "Slicing" I shamefully confessed. He then gave me one of these lessons which did produce some better shots, hitting balls into a net twenty feet away but make you feel awkward. As I recall he got me to turn my right shoulder into the ball until I seemed to be standing almost facing the hole as I swung through.

Chapter 4 – The Secret

At the end of my lesson the pro had some downtime, and we chatted - I think he was amazed that anyone would want to play indifferent golf for so many years yet still present as keen, cheery and cheeky about the game which had become his living.

"Can I give you a tip back?"I said. Before he could refuse I said "Do you know how you can cure a slice for £2.49? -simply buy a Tube-A-Grip bandage and put it on your left elbow; imagine if Jack Nicklaus's teaching pro Jack Grout had given him a bandage like that, it might have cured his flying elbow."

The pro looked at me straight and said with a slight smile "talk like that could reduce me to selling Mars bars!"

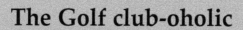

The Golf club-oholic

Chapter 1 – The Problem

My name is Frank and I am a golf-club-oholic.

That means I am addicted to the implements I deploy in my quest for golfing success and achievement. This is in direct contrast to those upwardly mobile types who collect golf club memberships at prestigious venues in their quest for power, at the expense of those who might play the courses more often and get proper benefit out of them.

Anyway for my own part I have known for the last 10 years or so that I'm a golf-club-oholic. Let's face it; you can only play with one set of 14 clubs at a time, or perhaps if pushed, sneak out on your own with a bag of about 25 clubs like the pros did in the hickory-shafted era. Ideally you only need about 7 clubs in a pencil bag; 3 Wood, 4-6-8 irons + pitching and sand wedges and putter). Thus you can walk the shortest way around the links with your hands nonchalantly in your pockets dreaming between shots and thus keeping your mind free of negative ideas. Then you can step back into the zone as you approach your ball, selecting a club from at most three possibilities, throw the lightweight bag down, go through your 5 second pre-shot routine and hit a decent shot every time.

A good analogy of the large/small set of golf clubs lies in the culinary staple – rice. Back in the day when I was at primary school, if I was loafing about before tea time I might be sent on an errand to the local grocers, occasionally for rice. In those days there were only two possibilities - long grain or round grain depending upon whether a rice pudding or a curry was in on the menu. Nowadays a request for rice contains more details - too many to remember white/brown/basmati/ Uncle Ben's and then you turn the corner in the supermarket to view an isle devoted to this basic foodstuff and your mind goes blank. After looking at all the types - saffron and others, you grab a bag of Uncle Ben's and then seize a tin of Ambrosia creamed rice to have at a quiet time when the rest of the household is out. You know that is not the type of rice you have been sent for, but the little impish voice in your head says to go for it, as the sensible part of your brain recoils under the plethora of rice possibilities. The same process and dilemma applies to golf clubs.

"The only time my prayers are never answered is on the golf course." - Billy Graham

As any addict will tell you, my problem started out innocently enough; I was given, at sporadic times, odd clubs for my starter set; a three wood, a five iron a seven iron (or mashie niblick as it described itself), and an uncompromising blade putter fashioned from a short bar of steel, the sort of putter that so far Scotty Cameron has yet to copy with an expensive alloy mix and sell for £300 to £400. My first putter had a hickory shaft which my Dad sawed down to suit my height and wound some sticky cloth tape round the end to fashion a vestigial grip.

I was ten or eleven at this time, and while my growing spurt from about 5 feet to nearly 6 feet came sometime in my mid-teens, I realised that I needed a sand wedge on account of the number of bunkers my ball visited. It seemed that the contours of my local course had been cunningly fashioned by the golf designer to guide my almost perfect shots into a disaster that took several blows to escape.

Chapter 2 – A Bit of History

My Dad didn't play much golf and his father's pre-2nd World War scratch man's set languished in a cupboard gathering dust, so I purloined the sand wedge or 'The Howitzer' as it proclaimed itself on the sole, and set off with a very heavy club several sizes too long for me. Somehow I hit a few good shots and slowly the other members of this set joined my bag until I purloined the leather bag itself and the narrow wheel 1950's caddy car to lug them. There were three wooden woods, driver, brassie and spoon, irons two to eight and a putter numbered nine. Add the Howitzer and an old hickory shafted aluminium headed mallet putter made by the Mills Company and there is my un-matched set. As an ardent Commando comic reader, I assumed the mallet putter was manufactured by the same organisation which made Mills bombs, mortars and grenades, but no; the howitzer connection had allowed my youthful imagination to run riot. Once I was hit on the head by the Mills putter when a friend was mucking about on the putting green outside the clubhouse and suddenly took a full backswing when I was standing close behind him. By the time I put my hand up to my forehead a huge bump had materialised but fortunately older members rushed out from the clubhouse with a cold compress on hearing my cries, including all the bad words I had learned. I still have that putter today but the head is slightly loose and I have an idea why that should be.

I grew up in my teens still playing that set, and as I got stronger I put them in a more modern bag with 14 integral tubes to protect the grips - it weighed a ton! Gradually I acquired a four wood which was more modern that the other woods, and a one iron manufactured by the same company, George Nicoll of Leven.

It was not until I was about 30, in the 1980s, that I saw that the professional at Duddingston Golf Club in Edinburgh, (at that time Jim Farmer, an ex Heart of Midlothian goalkeeper) had a sale which included a modern set of George Nicoll 'Pinsplitter' irons and wedges to which I added my relatively recently acquired one iron and four wood. Eventually when Nicoll's was on the point of going into liquidation, I obtained matching laminated one and two woods and my set was complete for the next 10 years. My only deviation during this period was the acquisition of the odd extra putter-a Titleist Dead Centre (a Ping Anser copy with sight lines on it) and an Acushnet Bulls Eye brass centre shafted putter with a flange low down on the back. Most of the time however I reverted to type and putted with a plain George Nicoll 'Zenith' blade putter and I used this set almost until the Millennium; the addiction was yet to come.

I had a brief flirtation with metal woods when they first came out, but pre titanium the heads were very heavy or small, or fairly inert unlike wood. I found they gave an extra 20 yards of length, but with my slice simply put me deeper into the rough, so for five seasons I teed off with an uncompromising one iron blade which kept me out of trouble but won me no prizes.

Chapter 3 – An innocent Start

In the mid 1990's, a second hand shop opened in Stockbridge in Edinburgh and as I walked by on a Saturday while buying groceries and cycling magazines (another obsession), I noticed old golf clubs and a few more modern ones. I soon got to know Chris Boyle, the friendly owner, and after buying and trying a set of Wilson Staff blades and finding them no better than those I had, found Chris happy to take them back less a tenner or so, following which I bought a set of Titleist DCI copies. Golf was about to explode with the Tiger Woods era, and players such as Davis Love III endorsed the real thing which at that time I could not afford; it was the era of 'knock off' clubs. The copies were quite good and seemed at their best on a cold day at the Strathclyde Park Driving Range at Hamilton where I used to go some lunchtimes from work. A blade iron can give you an awful jolt on a cold day when you mishit the ball, but these seemed to eliminate that flaw - not bad for £60. Around that time I went to a short-lived golf shop in Kirkcaldy and bought a semi mallet headed putter called a Phantom which I found good in the winter on grassy greens, on account of its greater than normal loft. It was many years before I discovered it was a copy of a Ping Zero. I eventually acquired a Ping Zero 2 but didn't like the offset head. I still have a Zero 4 which is much the same but am still on the lookout for a Mark 1 version, and I won't regard purchasing that as falling off the wagon! It is still a 'must have' along with, for some curious reason, an early set of Callaway Big Berth irons in copper beryllium.

When I took the DCI copies out on to the golf course I found the shafts were too short by an inch or so but were acceptable off a tee, and the heads, which were made of some zinc based alloy similar to that used to fashion Dinky and Corgi model toy cars, proved insubstantial. I traded them in for a Casio keyboard which I still have, as it boasted of good rhythms, a one finger chord facility for duffers like me (I'm a 24 handicap piano player) and it has an amazing church organ sound with cathedral sized reverb built in.

Chapter 4 – In Full Swing

By this time I was progressing at Silverfield, and managed to get my handicap down to 20. I had found another pop-up golf shop, like the one in Kirkcaldy and at Haymarket in Edinburgh, opposite the Edinburgh Golf Centre which survives to this day. The shop in question seemed to be run by two out-of-work ex-pros who talked the game and had several enticing second hand sets for sale. They had a set of Mega irons which seemed to be made of top quality steel and had muscle backs, like Ram clubs, which were played by some of the top pros of that era, but I had never heard of the brand although in retrospect I wish I had had the cash to buy them also. Instead I bought a set of Seve Ballesteros Slazenger irons -three to sand wedge, pressed them into service immediately and did well enough in the monthly medal to get my handicap cut. I also progressed quite far in the mixed foursomes competition with a decent lady partner. Seve's clubs were blades and difficult to play at five iron and below. I was using a hickory blade putter which I bought from Golf Classics who used to have a factory in St Andrews. It was a muscle backed Gem-type, similar to the one wielded many years before to good effect by Bobby Locke. It was very light so you could swing it with confidence, putt off the toe of the blade on the tricky downhill ones and bend the ball a bit to the right and left to counteract side slopes. Nowadays putters are great heavy things with wings like a sanitary towel advert, seemingly designed for a robotic straight hit which is impossible on the longer shots where your hands and arms describe an arc as you swing back and forth.

Back to the Seve blades; from six iron upwards they were superb. The scoring clubs for me, six and eight iron and pitching wedge were like jewels; the soles were fairly flat and they nipped the ball off the turf as I liked, and so apparently did six times Open winner Harry Vardon.

All I had to do was get the ball with 140 yards of the green and these clubs plus my putter did the rest, well level fives if you think that's acceptable.

I gave up the wooden woods and bought a Hippo titanium driver which had a much bigger head, and was easier to play than both wooden woods and the early metal woods which tended to have fairly small heavy heads which were hard to hit consistently. I had always been a keen golfer, but then started getting Golf Weekly as well as monthly magazines, and was soon seduced by all of the equipment. Equipment was forging ahead (what a terrible pun) in the wake of Tiger's dominance of the sport and the efforts of others to catch up, and so brand new clubs began to feature on my horizon. I was an advertiser's dream-anything with 'Tour' or 'Pro' inscribed upon it was for me, even if it resulted in an uncompromising club which I found aesthetically pleasing. Generally, after several hopeless rounds I realised it had a miniscule sweet spot that was hard for me to hit with any regularity, and a stiff shaft which tamed my quick 'Tom Watson', swing but also curbed the height and length of my shots. It took me some time to realise that a nice set of nearly new irons had been previously owned by a professional, or a low handicap golfer, who had to have the latest kit, and that these clubs invariably came with Dynamic Golf S400 shafts which were too strong for me, and gave me a rock like feel from each puny blow of mine at the ball. My 1982 Pinsplitter irons which I still possess had softer Accles & Pollock AP44 shafts which are no longer manufactured, nor are the beautiful stepless titanium Sandvic shafts which were swept away by graphite.

I was impressed by Fred Couple's exploits - I'd seen him at close quarters at the 1987 Muirfield Open effortlessly sweeping a tee shot 150 yards past his playing partner the cautious Roger Chapman. Ten years on Fred was a Major winner and even nowadays can find his way round the Masters' course in his 60s. He had been playing Lynx Clubs and so when the Black Cat Tour series of cavity back irons came out, I bought a set and added to it until I had one to nine irons, plus pitching, sand and lob wedges. That just left room for a driver and a putter but in time some of the long irons were left out of the bag to be replaced by woods, rescue clubs, chippers and other duffer aids. The thing about the Seve clubs was that below the six iron you had to hit them in the middle of the club; when you did it was a feeling like a hot knife through butter and the ball soared and landed sweetly. I had at one time sourced a two iron to match the set but it had quite a stiff shaft as only pros use these clubs. I did carry it once as I hit a great shot with it onto the green at a long par 3 at Whitecraigs in Glasgow and won the hole.

I think Freddie Couples went on to be sponsored by Maxfli and played their cavity blades for a bit. Eventually I acquired three sets of Maxfli irons to create the perfect duffers set, three to five cavity Revolution irons, and six to wedges Multilayer blades. In a rash moment when not playing the Seve blades I gave them to a friend who never returned them.

By this time the house was filling up and my obsession was becoming noticeable. The odd club or set sneaked into the house built up until clubs were propped up all around the walls of the spare bedroom. I was always looking for value and like a vinyl record collector I checked every shop, charity shop, club pro's shop and various websites. Soon I had amassed about a hundred putters of all types (except the pansy new ones) and about 35 sets of irons, mostly blades, but then I developed a sub obsession with Ping clubs which in earlier years I had discounted for their offset. I soon had early Karsten sets, named after the founder of the company (Karsten Solheim) followed by Ping Eyes, Eye 2s, Zings, Zing 2s, ISIs, I3Is, G2s, G5s, G10s, S59s, S56s and forged Ansers; oh yes and a few sets which were made of beryllium copper or nickel which had an extra great feel but the manufacturing process seemed to result in very toxic environmental pollution.

About this time I saw a Japanese website called Anser Freak where a man named Toshi explained and showed at length with copious photographs all the different Anser-type heel and toe balanced Ping putters he possessed. He also showed which bag of clubs he was taking out with him at the moment, and it seemed every time he had a different set of expensive Japanese clubs, He regularly used Honmas, an expensive brand once played by Lee Trevino, and Marumans, another top brand endorsed by Ian Woosnam in his prime.

I found golf club promiscuity quite normal by this stage and was not put off when I explained my 'hobby' to a golf-playing Professor of Maths at Edinburgh University who specialised in probability theory. He didn't bother to scribble out an equation on a blackboard for me but he did point out that I was not going to be a great golfer if I changed my clubs every week as it would only increase the already significant probability that my next shot would be a duff one.

My bible was 'The Guinness Guide to Golf Equipment' by David Graham, a multi golf Major winner and close friend and confident of Jack Nicklaus. He showed that there is little new in terms of golf equipment and in most cases increases in distance are due to improved ball construction and dynamics, the improved quality of shafts, particularly graphite, and also titanium headed woods.

When the Callaway Big Bertha came out it looked huge compared to the dimple headed metal Taylor Made driver which used to be used as a background when BBC TV News showed the results of a big golf tournament. There followed a Great Big Bertha and ever larger ones until 460 cc was fixed upon by the belated rule makers as the maximum size of head permitted. Nowadays a 440 cc head is a good compromise between the ease of hitting the largest size of driver against the aerodynamic drag from such a huge body.

For a while the faces of these brutes were made extra springy and hot, although that technology was later banned. I had a Mizuno driver for a while that was only about 330 cc but would go for miles if hit properly. Needless to say many of my shots ricocheted off the face at odd angles plunging me well into the rough, so after a while I gave it to my wee pal Danny who loved it and played it effortlessly as you would expect a tidy ball striker with a handicap of 6. Even after they were banned Danny would come out for a bounce game with me armed with the Mizuno.

Taylor Made then took over with big white headed adjustable drivers but I found the hit rather harsh, and have in recent years played Ping drivers, including G10. G15, G 20, G25, G30 and now G 400 which is just a joy (until the G 500 or whatever will inevitably come along).

I once went to a Cobra demonstration day and was 'fitted out' with an anti-slice draw-biased driver which I admit I hit well on the Duddingston Range where the event was held. However when I played with this new-fangled offset headed thing I found most of my shots were drawing into the left rough, an area of the course which I had little knowledge from years of slicing or fading balls into the right hand rough on the other side of the fairway. When I wasn't hooking the ball into left side deep rough I could, notwithstanding the manufacturer's claims and benign disposition to help guys like me, slice the ball just like before so that it entered rough on the right at a 90 degree angle from my initial intended direction. I think I gave away the Cobra to an unsuspecting friend with a mild slicing tendency but somehow never received any feedback reports; with his temper I suspect he broke it over his knee after a few rounds.

After that experience I just like a nice straight headed driver with no toe in or out and then it is down to me to stand properly to the ball aim deep into the left rough and trust the ball will bend to the right landing softly but safely on the right hand side of the fairway in a gentle parabola that I am pleased to call a power fade but pros, in teach-yourself-to-be-as-great-as-me books would dismiss as a banana slice.

So after 20 years of trying since I put down my beloved laminated wood no. two driver, I have found drivers I am happy with and are much easier to play than the tiny headed (150 cc) brassie with a metal shaft about four inches shorter than modern day drivers.

Similarly I loved Ping titanium headed metal woods of the type used for many years to great success by Miguel Angel Jimenez, the outlandish cigar smoking mullet-haired Spanish professional. I still have TISI Nos

3 and 5 woods which I had updated and re-shafted to great effect, but now realise 10 years on newer ones are better. I had a 13 degree three wood as well as the 15 degree one. The former was great off the tee but difficult for me off a tight fairway lie. I lent it to Danny and never saw it or its like again - I may have to buy an updated version sometime and feel I can do so without falling off the wagon.

Chapter 5 – Thinning Out the Collection

After 10 years I must have spent £10,000 on clubs, and while my handicap did go down to 18 at one point, much of that was to do with playing Silverfield's familiar fairways and deftly avoiding the trouble. I also kept a regular set of Ping woods and a putter I used until it went cold - only the irons changed every week or so to keep things interesting and justify my huge investment in equipment and the clutter it created at home.

About seven or eight years ago, three things happened which led me to ease off a bit. Firstly, we moved house and instead of having all my golf stuff cluttering a room, most of it had to be put up in the attic where the spare clubs languished for about five years. Secondly, my sister's terminal illness and the time it took to wind up her modest but scattered estate led me to give up membership at Silverfield, with the result that I played a lot less golf.

I still popped into golf shops, as I mostly went to the driving range rather than have a full round of golf. Each time I had to run the gauntlet of all the golf equipment, just like you have to do at a supermarket to obtain a pint of milk - you are intentionally diverted past all on show and all the special offers. I bought fewer sets of irons, unless they were in my view dead bargains, when it was a shame to see them languishing unbought. I purchased a few new putters I later found were still in the shrink wrapping they came in and had never been played. The third and final catalyst came when my son was due to go on a school trip to Malawi which involved helping teach at an orphanage. The cost of the trip was not inconsiderable and on top of that each boy was expected to raise about £500 to give as a donation to the cause. My son came up rather belatedly with ideas such as asking famous people to do a work of art on a postcard then auction them off at an exhibition, or washing cars. I told him the first idea would take the best part of a year to do and he had about 3 months, and as for the second he would have to wash a lot of cars at £5 to £10 a time, having had little or no inclination or experience of washing any cars in the past, which included his own father's vehicle.

I was damned if we were going to fork out the £500, and didn't want to send the lame round robin to work mates about another worthy event, where something daft was going to be done in the name of charity, then directing these jaded souls to a JustGiving web page. I decided if the boy could help me get all the golf equipment out of the attic, and help me catalogue it in the hope I could offer clubs to a few golfing pals at knock-down prices.

I made a list, which frankly shocked me about the amount and quantity of golf clubs I had amassed. I think the same psychological process is deployed by Weight Watchers and Drug Rehab Centres to get you to make a diary of what you have consumed over a period, then reflect upon it in the cold light of day.

Out of the 35 sets of irons, I held back about a dozen which I felt were indispensable, and covered the main aspects of my golfing needs. Business was slow but I flogged two sets to a workmate, two clubs to my boss and another set to the owner of my favourite chip shop. Within a month I had raised the £500 and felt a warm glow compared to the gloom and guilt when going up to the attic for the Christmas decorations and seeing all these beautiful objects gathering dust. It was a cathartic moment which the old pro at Silverfield never had. He kept old stock for years and still wanted top dollar for it. I think when he handed over to a younger guy he paid a nominal price for it all and junked most of it.

I used to love visiting the Golf Trap in Dundee, a shop crammed with new and many second hand clubs taken as trade ins. I bought a lot of Ping stuff, there putters and woods mostly and got rid of irons that were too difficult to play, like Mizuno Blades with X stiff shafts! I suggested to the owner that he put a lot of the stuff on E bay and clear a lot of it away, but he seemed reluctant to do so and one day when I returned to the street it was shut, and its precious haphazard contents had gone. I still miss the thrill of wandering up and down the narrow shop selecting clubs, reading the labels on the shafts and checking prices. It must have been like the rush a drug addict gets or a gambler when the wheel or the horses are running, or ants are crawling a wall oblivious to the amounts staked on which will be first to the ceiling.

So I had met my target, but had offered lots of clubs which no one seemed to want. I then noticed that near to me was Golfclubs4cash. I visited their warehouse premises at Bilston, outside Edinburgh and found it crammed with all manner and age of clubs from the latest to stuff so old even I wouldn't want to buy. After summoning up the courage, I made a few visits and sold £1,500 worth of clubs and bags and bought a few things in exchange including an electric trolley. The only New Year's Resolution I have kept was to give up smoking and I haven't smoked since I was fourteen. As a young man I resolved never to get engaged or married, but these personal promises were broken soon after.

As the years swept by and my golfing prowess plateaued out around the 18-24 mark, I resolved never to buy an electric trolley, but I now have a top-of-the-range model which folds up very neatly. The young salesman at Golfclubs4cash said it was designed to fit into the front 'boot' of a Porsche 911; I will have to take his word for that. All I can say is that is does make this unfit old addict get round the course a bit quicker by dragging me along, and I have been able to sneak it into the house without it being too obtrusive. It was a really good feeling to get rid of that old stock; of course I made a bit of a loss on it, but I was pleased that some items were priced at more than I paid for them! While I have a nice bag which fits and matches the caddy car and have mostly kept to the same set, I could not help but notice the driving range was selling off old clubs which they had taken in as trade-ins at ridiculous prices. I bought a lovely set of Ping Eyes for £30 and used them to great success one day playing with friends at Shaw Park Course at Alloa. The next time I turned up with a set of Tommy Armour irons which cost £15 but did the job though they could do with new grips.

Chapter 6 – Stable but not Cured

I am still therefore a bit of a golf-club-oholic. I'm not like the alcoholic who told me after a few months' counselling he was much better, in that he had stopped drinking two bottles of vodka a day, and was no longer going to pubs and getting into fights, but instead he was living quietly at home, watching day-time TV and drinking **just** twelve cans of super strength lager a day. This did seem to me to be a full-time job. I reckon I am pretty much cured and have plenty of clubs to see me out. I have gathered a few more sets to sell off, though I may replace one with a newer second hand set; that's surely permissible?

The last time I was at the driving range, I did see a nice 13 degree Ping G400 3 wood which would go with my driver, and I still scan the second hand stuff for a set of gold coloured Callaway Big Bertha irons - God knows why as I used to duff the steel ones plenty through the fairway, despite hitting good tee shots.

Like the alcoholic I just mentioned, I feel that I am pretty much cured. I am open to offers for most of my equipment, and often respond to calls from keen friends or young people starting out in this great game, giving them a set or individual clubs. However, niggling at the back of my head is this impish voice which echoes the manufacturer's blurb that this club or that putter will transform your game. It's not my fault I am a 24 handicapper, sometimes the clubs get in the way! I remain optimistic that out there is a driver, a five wood, four, six and eight irons, a wedge and a putter, where all you have to do is hang on to the handles and let the clubs do the work. Surely they would be easier to design than a driverless car? I could load them into a pencil bag, leave the electric trolley at home, and walk the most economical way round the course in a ridiculously small number of strokes. It's all a matter of finding the right set of clubs that will produce a synergy to transcend my slice, lack of length, indifferent short game and poor course management. When that happens I can give away all the other clubs, well, apart from a few to keep for old time's sake; Grandfather's set, my 'new' Pinsplitters, my copper Ping Eye 2s, the nickel Ping ISIs, the Mizunos with the 5.5 Rifle shafts and my Ping s56s which are currently in my bag, oh and perhaps about twenty putters. I'm not drug-free as they say, but I am stable and perhaps the probability of the next golf shot not being a duff one has reduced exponentially.

PS - In the bag currently are a set of Benross Compressor Type R Taylor Made-type irons with slits in the soles for improved weight distribution. According to the label they were £419 when first priced but I got them in their wraps for just £74! I don't need to hit great shots to get value out of them but they feel good. I am trying to lead a normal golfing life but can still be tempted.

My Favourite Golf Books

The thing about golf is you need a lot of stuff; clubs, bag, special shoes, lurid golf apparel - (it's never been hi-jacked by the fashion industry in the way that streetwear and other sports like athletics have), golf trolley, manual, electric, or even a single or two seater buggy, and, perhaps a few lessons too.

Over fifty years of playing I have only gone for lessons a few times. I imagine most driving instructors teach the same stuff. There's a Highway Code to follow and test routes and set manoeuvres to bone up on. True there are PGA professionals and a degree of similarity about their teaching these days - hit it as hard as you can and we'll worry about accuracy later because all you'll need are 4 wedges to get out of the trouble you've put yourself in.

Some teaching pros are very good and do little to change your swing but give you a few thoughts to take away with you which may resonate for the whole season. Like the time I turned up all keen on the 2nd of January at the Braid Hills Golf Range as 6 inches of snow precluded golf elsewhere. The golf range was closed but the professional, Colin Brooks, appreciating my keenness, gave me a free impromptu lesson and took a photograph of my position at address, and in comparing it to Nick Faldo's set up flatteringly suggesting we were of similar build. I looked at this print all season and the tips he gave stayed with me for a long time. Others just push you about, and give you an awkward grip, stance and posture, but say you must persevere with this, the only true way. Even when the advice is good, if you don't play immediately and try to put it into practice on the normal undulating slopes of a course, as opposed to the flat consistency of the practice mat, you forget most of it.

Soon you turn to the golf book, something you can access at any time, even in the night when you wake up sweating with some dreadful swing thought, or how you lost a 10 shot lead in the Masters by yipping your way home in 40 strokes, and that was just the putts!

I must have been about 12 when I was given for a birthday or a Christmas present **"Teach Yourself Golf" by Dr J C Jessop** who had been a keen amateur. It was just one of a series of small volumes which hoped to teach you a variety of sports and other activities just like the modern" **** for Dummies" series.

This book was first published in 1950 when centre-shafted putters were still illegal and stymies ruled in match play. It had been a popular volume as my copy was a new edition published in 1960 but still looked charmingly old fashioned.

There were beautiful line drawings of a middle-aged man swinging a brassie (2 wood) or a blaster (sand wedge) and much of the advice was simple and sensible. I go back to that book like a comfort blanket not so much for tips but for reassurance that nothing much is new in golf and it's the basics which count.

A sign perhaps of a reduction in golf over the years is the dearth of the 4 picture golf tips which used to appear in Sunday Newspaper sports sections over the summer months. I cut them out and collected them, and sometimes they appeared in a whole book. Later on there was a good series of PGA books on par 3s, par 4s and par 5s as well as other aspects of the game.

I read a lot of golf biographies but there seemed to be little in the way of a common theme, other than in most cases the subject started playing at an early age and no doubt had put in the necessary 10,000 hours by an early age (which I didn't). Many had fathers who were golf pros like Sandy Lyle, Sam Torrance and Peter Alliss to name a few, or had Tiger Woods Dads (like Tiger Woods). Others were largely self-taught, like Bubba Watson, Seve Ballesteros and Lee Trevino. Some oozed natural talent which they wasted or didn't nurture like John Daly and others worked hard and arguably over-achieved, like Padraig Harrington or Ian Poulter - no shame in that. Their life stories as told in these books are short, and the rest is golf my way; the grip, baseball-type with the hands close together, interlocking like Tiger Woods or Jack Nicklaus - (coincidence?) or Vardon-type with the hands more integrated. Then there is stance: hitting the ball off the front foot or with the ball between the feet or even off the back foot. So on it goes there is a world of difference between the carefully guru-modelled swing of Nick Faldo to the unorthodox styles of Lee Trevino or Jim Furyk.

The best thing to do is choose someone your own size whose style you like and whose book explains the basics clearly with great illustrations.

Step forward **Tommy Armou**r, the Silver Scot who emigrated to America, won three Majors then had a long and successful career as a teaching pro. His books still stand the test of time aided by simple line drawings which focus the reader on the points being made. They don't distract you like the books which show photographs of the resort-type sunny backdrops, or the distracting clothing worn by many golfers. Tommy's books are short and none more useful than "**A Round of Golf with Tommy Armour**" (first published in 1959) where he plays in a 9 hole foursome and suggests how golfers if differing abilities might tackle the holes. "**How to Play Your Best Golf All the Time**" is his classic text first published in the 1950s and republished many times. I got a lot out of that book but sadly playing my best all the time has rarely troubled the scorers!

Recently I acquired the delightful "**Classic Golf Tips**" by Tommy Armour a posthumously-published collection of one page tips complete with line drawings and a wonderful Foreword by his enigmatic grandson and touring golf pro Tommy Armour III. He was a streaky player who won only a couple of PGA events, but had very fast hands into the shot which made him an effortless long hitter.

Many golfers' books skimp in the equipment section nowadays, most are sponsored by one of the leading firms and these allegiances often change over the years sometimes with disastrous consequences but others like Justin Rose have stayed loyal to the one manufacturer throughout their career - namely Taylor Made although he moved to Honma in January 2019.

Fashions change and the old books which advocated 4 woods, 9 irons and a putter were replaced with pros

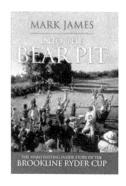

Like **Mark James** who carried a driver, 12 irons (1-9 + pitching), sand and lob wedges and a putter. The introduction of hybrid wood/iron clubs which together with the lowering of the loft of irons led to 1-3 and sometimes also the 4 iron being phased out and replaced by more wedges. These cover the gap from 45-60 degrees of loft for those delicate shots played on approach to the green from pitch and run, to lob or flop shots as popularised by Phil Mickelson.

Most books will tell you to buy good quality clubs and get them fitted out to suit your height and the length of your arms and the right stiffness of shaft depending upon how fast you can swing the club.

Unless you make copious notes as you read these books and constantly refer to them you will forget most of the advice and it will all become a blur of contradicting philosophies.

Ultimately you have to find what works best for you. It doesn't matter is you are stiff and straight legged like the legendary RDBM (Right Down the Bloody Middle) Ronnie Shade or have a swing with twists and turns like Jim Furyk; all you have to do is bring the club straight onto the ball at the vital millisecond of impact.

So how have I evolved into the duffer I am after subjecting myself to a lifetime of conflicting theories?

I play my drives opposite my front heel and a high tee to match the deep face of the titanium club.

I play irons with the ball opposite the middle of my feet and chip the ball with my feet turned to face the hole at an angle bringing the club smartly down opposite my back foot. I putt off the front foot. Maybe that is too many variables. I do duff my irons a lot taking turf before ball but think I must sway during the swing-must check my swing in a shadow next time we have some sunshine!

The reassuring thing about reading books written or ghosted for them by great golfers is that they all lost far more often than they won and all have played a few holes so badly in their careers that it gives you hope.

Golf videos are helpful too but you can't watch them and practise at the same time. A video of your own swing shocks you like the first time you hear your recorded voice or gulp at a ghastly photo taken in a split second which seems to depict you at what you think is your worst but makes you think this is probably the "normal" others seen you all the time!

So golf books are worth dipping into - ignore the stuff that doesn't or won't work for you. Look out some classic titles and marvel at how **Lady Margaret Scott** became Ladies Champion in a full skirt and matching jacket, how a one legged man could hit a full shot without falling over and how the cool guys in the 1950s played without taking the cigarette out of their mouths - I bet they didn't have prolonged pre-shot routines otherwise they would get in the way of a 60-a-day habit. Joyce Wethered, a leading amateur in the 1920s and 30s whose style was much admired by the leading professionals of the day played immaculate golf in a 3/4 length suit, starched collar and sensible brogues.

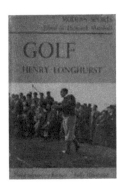

Other great golf books have been written by journalists like **Bernard Darwin**, a grandson of the famous naturalist, **Herbert Warren Wind**, the eloquent American writer and the late great **Henry Longhurst** who was the elderly commentator on BBC golf until Peter Alliss became old enough. Another of my favourites is '*Golf*' by

Henry Longhurst, first Edition 1937 published by J.M. Dent & Sons. The author was golf correspondent for the *Sunday Times* for 45 years, and during the 2nd World War he was MP for Acton. He died in 1978 and was inducted into the World Golf hall of fame in September 2017.

I have never had a caddie all the years I have played but thanks to Henry's book of essays simply called 'Golf' from 1937 I know how to tip a caddie. You give "a good one a shilling and sixpence, unless there is a rule in the club stipulating that the tip shall not exceed a shilling." I bet they had such a rule back in the day at Muirfield. Since Longhurst stated the caddie's primary duty "and the one he often shirks" is to replace the turf you have taken with your shot I would have had to have given him more than a florin given the number and depth of turfs I take duffing my way around the course.

 Once I started collecting golf clubs in the 1990s, the book I enjoyed most and wish was updated is **The Guinness guide to golf Equipment** by two-time Major winner **David Graham. He** was a tough Australian professional, friend and confident of Jack Nicklaus. As well as playing golf to a high standard and sinking some notable long putts to win a US Open and US PGA, Graham had learned his trade as a club pro-he could make replica golf clubs as Gary Player testifies in the Foreword to the book. Graham's chapters on shafts and grips are very informative. I start with a clubhead I like the look of, that sits well and is not too clunky then I make sure the shafts suit me-5.5 Rifle, Callaway Uni Flex or the late lamented Ackles and Pollock AP 44s.

True Temper is an excellent make but S300s or S400s are too stiff and heavy for my puny swing speed nowadays although a firm graphite shaft suits my woods well on account of the brisk switch at the top of my swing between backswing and downswing.

A read through Graham's book reveals that little in golf is new-metal headed clubs were made over 100 years ago as was the centre-shafted Schenectady putter. To my mind the only true innovations in the last 60 years are Ping-type heel- and- toe weighed putters, graphite shafts and titanium heads for woods.

For irons it's not the modern clubhead that makes the ball go further it's the ball itself followed by the shaft. Irons are more forgiving but there is nothing like the feeling of flushing a forged blade 5 iron -a Mizuno for example and seeing the ball fly high straight and true. That's a rare event in my case and I would have more consistent efforts off a tee at any rate with a Big Bertha iron which has a large undercut cavity at the back of the head and a heavy sole to get the ball flying high and squeezing the best out of miss-hits-trouble is I find them too ungainly off tight fairway lies or hacking my way out of the rough-I think they were designed specifically to play off Bermuda grass which is common in the US and warmer climes and makes the ball sit up invitingly. They're not so good on wet worn bedraggled Scottish grass.

Loft and lie of clubs are important considerations too and Ping's colour code marked on the back of each iron guide helps. After years of playing I am best with Blue-1 degree upright but can get away with Black which is standard. I have played with red-I degree flat and white 2 degrees upright with limited success. If your shots are unaccountably hooking to the left the lie of the club is too upright whereas slicing to the right may be your irons are too flat. You can get more irons bent slightly to adjust the lies and lofts to suit you.

One of the oddities in the Putters section of David Graham's book is a sketch of a 'backwards' putter which had a straight shaft and a cast head with a wryneck designed for those who putted with their hands behind the ball- a technique which most professionals do not advocate. Eventually after some years, being intrigued by the design I tracked a Taylor Made one down. It is an ugly looking thing and must have been in vogue for about 10 seconds in the late 1980s to early 1990s. Needless to say I only played one round with it and holed nothing!

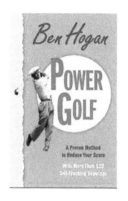

Having grown up in the long shadow of **Jack Nicklaus** I have acquired a few of the many books issued during his long career. They are still worth a look today as he was the role model for today's tall powerful hitter and the master of the 1 iron a club that Lee Trevino joked by raising to the heavens during a thunderstorm and declared "Even God can't hit a 1 iron!" Nowadays most of the low irons have been phased out of the set which often starts with a 5 backed up with a number of rescue clubs but if you are able to compare your new 5 iron with a pre-war 3 iron you will find they are about the same loft 24 degrees whereas at one time a 5 iron had a loft of 30 degrees-no wonder the newer club can go further.

Among the most revered books are those ones by **Ben Hogan** such as **'Power Golf'** from 1948 which clearly pointed to the future and the Golden Years of Palmer, Nicklaus and Player. Hogan was an enigmatic figure with his own style, a fervent practiser who with great determination recovered from a serious road accident in 1949 to win many more tournaments including the 1953 Open at Carnoustie the only time he entered. Plant your left foot to start the downswing and flick your wrists in the hitting zone to get maximum distance were classic tips for generations of golfers following.

Before Hogan the dominant force in golf was **Byron Nelson** whose classic book **Winning Golf** made him enough money to retire early from the tour after winning 10 consecutive events, and enable him to set up a successful cattle ranch. Despite being a haemophiliac he lived a long life, became a notable teacher of the game and founded arguably the best memorial tournament - the Byron Nelson Classic where for many years he congratulated the winning player as he walked off the last green - the respect this modest man received from all competitors was palpable.

Since I played **Henry Cotton** branded irons for many years I sought out his books and was not disappointed. **This Game of Golf** (1949), **My Swing** (1952), **Golfing Techniques in Pictures** (1957) and **Golf The Picture Story of The Golf Game** (1965) all depict the immaculately -turned out 3-time Open winner- a sartorial style with which I could not compete but I bonded with the way he preferred to change at his car rather than in the clubhouse though in the era he played professionals were often not welcome in club houses at tournaments they played, by the so-called 'gentlemen' members.

Cotton's books are full of photographs of men playing in plus fours or trousers with turn-ups and V-necked sweaters and ties, with the women in sensible pleated skirts and long-sleeved cardigans. Cotton does show a photo of him in large boxer shorts to give an idea of his posture when showing his wrist action.

In **My Swing,** Cotton eschews the use of line drawings which went before, and follows the lead set by Bobby Jones by using a series of high speed photos to produce flick-book like images of his swing with each club-driver, brassie and spoon woods, 1 to 9 irons and an extra-long-shafted cleek with an even shallower face than a 1 iron for playing into the wind. The series was completed by images of his pitching and sand wedges, and his putter.

 *My Swing* **by Henry Cotton** was published 1952 by Country Life Ltd. Sir Thomas Henry Cotton MBE won the Open in 1934, 1937 and 1948. His second round of 65 in the 1934 Open was celebrated by the issue of the Dunlop 65 ball. He was born in 1907 and died in 1987 aged 80. He played in the Ryder Cup in 1929, 1937 and 1947 and captained the team in 1947 and 1953. After a career in golf he became a successful golf architect. He loved the high life, was always immaculately dressed, and was driven about in his Rolls Royce by a butler. For many years I played George Nicoll of Leven irons endorsed by Henry Cotton.

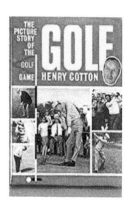 When my daughters were of primary school age a perfect holiday day was spent driving to St Andrews. I watched players on the Old Course wistfully as we parked on the West Beach car park and organised our picnic. After a bare foot run along the beach like the 'Chariots of Fire' film (only much slower), the girls would go with

their mother to the swimming pool and I would trawl the golf shops for second hand clubs and visit the now sadly departed Quarto Books which was situated next to the first tee of the Old Course. I started buying golf books particularly older ones which described the finesse and skill of the game rather than the modern thrash- and- wedge game.

The charming **Principles of Golf by M J Astle** (1923) with wonderful illustrations **by Miss Marjorie Bates** is a joy. Twelve chapters and 109 pages cover all aspects of the game and are accompanied by superb illustrations of a moustachioed middle aged man in a suit with 3 buttons on the jacket, turn-ups on the trousers, stout brogues and a tie depict how it is done; I must try that mode of address sometime perhaps we have all got out of shape wearing polo shirts or even worse - T shirts!

All About Golf: How to Improve Your Game by Bert Seymour (1924) is from a similar era written by a professional who won the 1921 News of the World matchplay championship. His photographs show the author in plus fours, a cardigan, tie and flat cap. He appears to swing a little stiffly and it may be that some of the swing shots are posed. He advocated a 9 club set comprising driver, brassie, spoon plus a cleek, mid iron, mashie, mashie niblick, niblick and putter i.e 1-3 woods + 1, 4, 5, 7, wedge irons. There is a very genteel but well-meaning chapter entitled "Golf for Ladies". Interestingly in contrast to the modern fashion of large taper- less grips for putters Seymour writes enthusiastically about having no grip on his putter and using a pendulum swing which involved flexing the wrists-again a modern no-no. What does endear Bert to me is in summarising the 12 elements of putting he says at Number (2) "Do not waste much time taking the line of the putt as that admits an element of doubt." I would love all contemporary players to bear that in mind.

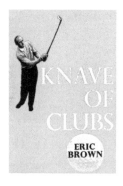

Although my dad didn't play much golf, my Grandfather had been a scratch man and dad followed the game in the sports pages when I imagine much more space was devoted to the game than nowadays. Consequently he was a big **Eric Brown** fan. The first top golfer to come from Bathgate in West Lothian, the former railway man who shot to fame with numerous tournament wins and stellar performances in the Ryder Cup, and one who wore his dour Scots credentials on his sleeve. He was a great party animal and regularly shared a dram with rising star Sean Connery. Brown's '**Knave of Clubs'** is well worth a read, particularly the stories of his various championship wins and dramas. His putting stroke with a simple blade displays the now unfashionable wristy action.

Another grumpy hero of mine from the past was Bobby Locke. He won 4 Open Tournaments and 15 PGA tournaments in America and countless trophies in his native South Africa. He coined the phrase 'you drive for show and putt for dough'. He was an excellent putter and could impart spin of the ball to minimise the break

on putts much to the consternation of his opponents who tried to find a line by watching Locke putt. A big man who walked and played slowly and deliberately he drew the ball from right to left as opposed to my left to right slicer's trajectory. Most of all he putted with a hickory-shafted muscle-back blade putter of the Gem variety. He is the anthemia to all modern golf but shows you don't need to follow the vogue to score well.

Notwithstanding his unfashionableness his book, **Bobby Locke on Golf** published in 1953 still commands high prices and is an excellent treatise on his unique style.

***Bedrock Principles of golf* by W W Lowe** first Edition 1937, published by Collins. Walter Lowe was a great all-round athlete excelling in athletics, cricket, football, skating, skiing and tobogganing as well as golf. He describes the growth of the game from the 1890s when a set of 7 clubs was commonplace to accompany the gutty ball and bemoans the need to lengthen courses with the advent of the rubber-cored ball. His suggestions about abolishing stymies and advocating the reduction of time-wasting are refreshingly modern, so he was ahead of his time

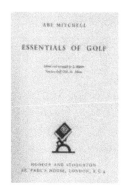

Essentials of Golf **by Abe Mitchell** published in 1927 by Hodder and Stoughton. Abe Mitchell was reckoned to be one of the best ball strikers of his era but never won a major. He played in 3 Ryder Cups 1929-1933 but was too ill to take his place in the 1927 match. In 1933 he beat his opponent 9 and 8. Having taught Sir Samuel Ryder to play golf in the 1920s he was rewarded when that businessman put up the money to inaugurate the biennial match play competition between the US and UK and Irish (later European) professionals by using a likeness of Abe Mitchell as the golfer on top of the Ryder Cup. Abe's book is full of wise words "Great musicians spend countless hours in acquiring and perfecting their technique before they pass on to interpretation, and the golfer should take a lesson from them." This sage text by a well-respected professional in his day contains an invaluable chapter on escaping the stymie and the author waxes nostalgically on the advantages of putting with the inert gutty ball compared to the over-liveliness of that Haskell thing. He advocates the use of a hickory shafted aluminium headed mallet (Mills-type) putter of about 10 ounces in weight - "it is a mistake to use a light club", or a putting cleek with too much loft. Hard core stuff before the introduction of steel shafts and the sand wedge, so plenty of explanation about the uses of driver, brassie and spoon + 1-3 irons mashie and mashie- niblick.

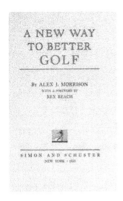

A New Way to Better Golf by **Alex J Morrison** First Published 1932, cheap Edition August 1935 published by William Heinemann. The author taught principally in the United States and convinced Babe Ruth, the great baseball slugger and famous left-hander to play golf right handed – no doubt it would be easier to sell him some clubs. Alex was one of four brothers who became golf professionals. His main claim to fame is that he taught Henry Picard, who in turn taught Jack Grout who became Jack Nicklaus's long-term teacher. Alex was born in 1896 and although his date of death is not clear he taught into the 1950s. In the last chapter of the book the learned author critiques well known players of the day, but concludes despite differences in their swings they reach the hitting area in the same way. He describes his long held criticism of Bobby Jones' muscular golf and concludes KEEP YOUR CHIN BACK.

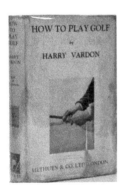

How to Play Golf by **Harry Vardon** first published 1912, 21st Edition 1934. The inventor of the 'Vardon Grip' and winner of the Open 6 times - you get it all in this book. "It is always as well to carry two drivers – one fairly stiff and the other moderately supple." P. 42 The theory being one will play better when you are filled with exuberance and the other when you are more subdued. Funnily enough I have reached the same conclusion recently myself. "Professionals have long since come to the conclusion that the wooden clubs played by many indifferent players are too long.

It is easier to control a short driver than a long one;"
P. 44 On building a tee with a pinch of damp sand: "The
ball should be just perched on the sand [on the tee] so
that none of the latter can be seen to be sitting up clear
of the ground supported by nothing. That optical
delusion gives you confidence to hit it well." P. 47
Collars are by no means unimportant details of dress"
p.50 they should be no more than an inch high. Vardon
bemoans the passing of the gutty ball in favour of the
Haskell rubber ball and waxes lyrical how it took
the skill out of the game and brought professionals
back to the level of the talented amateur rather like
when the Titleist Pro VI was introduced and lesser
known professionals found the benefits of the ball
quicker than the stars. Vardon lived from 1870 to 1937
and together with J H Taylor and James Braid was
part of the great Triumvirate. Vardon's other great pearl
of wisdom was that shirt "collars are by no means
unimportant details of dress and should be no more
than an inch high". That would go nicely with the
3 piece suit and tie then.

He won 6 Opens 1896, 1898, 1903, 1911 and 1914 and
the US Open in 1900. Presumably his last 2 Opens were
won with that new-fangled ball!

HARRY
WEETMAN

100 ACTION
PHOTOGRAPHS
OF
HARRY
WEETMAN
IN PLAY

The Way to Golf by **Harry Weetman**
First Edition 1953 published by Ward,
Lock & Co Ltd

The author was the longest hitter
of the golf ball in Britain at the time
and Match Play Champion in 1951.
Seven times a member of the Ryder
Cup team (1951-63) and captain in
1965 opposite Byron Nelson. After
a description of his techniques a
copious photographs of him playing

in a thick woolly scarf the author concludes with a heartening tale of contemporary golf. "One of the brightest aspects has been the tremendous strides made by the artisan movement.....In writing that I exclude Scotland, of course, where artisan sections do not exist as far as I know. The reason is that in most parts of Scotland everyone can play golf at a very cheap rate." pp. 150-151.

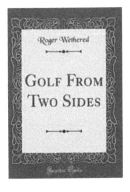

Golf from Two Sides **by Roger and Joyce Wethered** Second Edition 1925 published by Longmans, Green & Co

These brother and sister toffs were both excellent golfers and never dirtied their hands by turning pro. Roger was born in 1899 and died in 1983; Joyce was born in 1901 and died in 1997. In 1937 she married Major Sir John Heathcoat Amory. Bobby Jones and Walter Hagen both admired her play - Jones saying "the most gifted player I have ever seen", while Hagen said "she hit her shots crisply-firm and strong like a man...not to detract from her charm as a gracious young sportswoman."

The book covers all elements of the golf game from the male and female perspectives. Chapter VIII describes the virtues of wooden putters, but Ms Wethered clearly preferred the steel headed cleek despite the inconsistencies between such clubs due to each being individually forged at that time. There is a fetching series of photos on Ms Wethered putting in a threequarter length skirt suit, starched collar, sensible brogues and a proper hat. In Chapter XII Roger waxes lyrical on golf at Oxford University since the Great War and describes the joys of bunking off a day's lectures to golf at Huntercombe.

The learned author describes the skill of a fellow student Cyril Tolley who won one Varsity match 9 and 7 by playing to level 4s and being able to contemplate driving the ball 240 yards. He later became Major Cyril Tolley MC, winning his medal in the First World War, and commanded a company of the Royal Sussex Regiment in the Second. He was British Amateur Golf Champion in 1920 and 1929 and second to Bobby Jones in 1930. He won the French Open in 1924 and 1928.

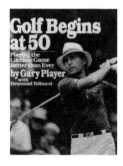

Golf Begins at 50 by Gary Player, 1988 published by Simon and Schuster, New York. This book was written when he was 53, and had already won three Majors on the Champions Tour following his nine Majors in Open events, the last of which was when he was 43 years of age. He was therefore in all probability the most qualified individual to write on the topic of golf for 50 year olds. The book is a mix of guidance on lifestyle, mental strength and exercise, and their relationship to golf. The sections on golf improvement which have been of most assistance to me include those on percentage shots, problem shots made easy, and how to turn three shots into two. Lifestyle advice includes diet (fewer fatty foods for me), exercise for which the author is famed, and mental strength, including concentration, and goal visualisation and management. Lots of useful photographs and diagrams follow the usual style of his books – heavy on illustrations, light but effective on words. One of his other very useful books for me was **Gary Player's Golf Clinic**, first published by DBI books Inc. in 1981. This is a series of around 600 cartoon-style tips, first published by Beaverbrook Newspapers Ltd in the Daily Express between 1973 and 1980. These two and three part tips provided weekly golfing advice for the masses, and are fondly remembered by many. The two illustration example shown below deals with long bunker shots, and as usual addresses just a couple of key points, in this case shortening your grip, and aiming for the top of the ball.

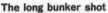

The long bunker shot

In conclusion

These are some of the wonderful golf books I have enjoyed. Golf, like history, is best considered in retrospect. I get enough tips from contemporary professionals and one hears of their A-list lifestyles. It is a far cry from when Gary Player came from South Africa in the 1950's to try and break into the British Tour, before becoming one of the Big Three in the US alongside Jack Nicklaus and Arnold Palmer. In the beginning he occasionally had to sleep in a bunker.

If I had to choose a few books out of all of the ones I have read, the following three (in no particular order) would be high on my list.

- **Teach Yourself Golf** by Dr J C Jessop
- **How to Play Your Best Golf all of the Time** by Tommy Armour
- **Golf begins at 50** by Gary Player

So what are my conclusions? I have enjoyed reading many contradictory tomes and seen plenty of rubbish written. Keep It Simple Sucker - having 30 odd swing points to check as Sam Torrance once claimed is way beyond me, and perhaps is the reason he didn't win a Major, as he had all the talent (and a great teacher in his father); maybe he had too much going on in his head.

Keep a few of your favourite books to hand and consult them from time to time. A golf lesson with a video of your swing to take home is a good way of reminding yourself of how you can do things properly. Play every shot as if it matters but most of all, relax, flex the knees slightly, waggle the toes, smile, and sweep the ball away ending on a high finish; the rest is detail.

Characters I have met on the Golf Course

Mike Lindsay
A member at Murrayfield and friend of my Dad with whom I worked at the North of Scotland Hydro-Electric Board. He was the Secretary of the Hydro-Board pension fund which did not impress a 23 year old young blade with a lightning fast swing. He was very kind and used to drive me in his maroon Austin 1800 to Gullane Golf Course in East Lothian once a month to play in a Winter League over their no 3 Course. While many will say it is much the easiest of the three Gullane Links courses, it took me all my time to play at 8 am on a Saturday after a late night on the town. My golf, though promising, was fairly erratic, and it was Mike (all 24 handicap of him) who suggested I shorten my swing! The rest is history. Tom Watson's brisk tempo was my ideal but sometimes I was so quick I forgot to take a backswing. I certainly never paused at the top!

The Old Man of the Sea
I was paired up with two straggly bearded ancients once when waiting for a game at Silverknowes. They were in their 60's and I would be about 35. I called one of them the Old Man after the Hemmingway novel as he had a long white beard and captain's hat. I swear he wore a duffel coat but that would be an exaggeration. More importantly he carried an illegal adjustable iron and a putter. His mate had the yips and possibly

Parkinson's disease. They were harmless old blokes, but eventually I had to turn away when they played as their styles, such as they were, totally put me off my swing! The Old man didn't need a golf bag and just stuck a few balls in his pockets, but the rough was thick that summer and I think I had to help him out when he ran out of balls on the back nine!

Billy Casper
Another pick up partner at Silverknowes in the mid-sixties when I was still at school. Not the real Billy Casper but a kindly old boy lived near the course and had just retired. He was a tidy golfer, very patient with me and wielded a centre-shafted Titleist Bulls Eye putter to good effect. He explained it was all in the wrists and said how much he admired Billy Casper, who to my young eyes was a rather tubby non-descript figure on the Tour. It is all a far cry from all that rigid triangle stuff and putters with wings we have nowadays. I realise now that when we played, Billy Casper was at the height of his powers as a prolific winner on the PGA Tour and winner of 3 major championships. His short game and putting were renowned. I still use a bit of wrists in my putting stroke to this day in his honour, but I realise that it is terribly old fashioned and frowned upon.

Happy Howden
He was a regular face at Silverknowes and stood out with his bald head, white cap, immaculate golf clothes and pristine white shoes. He had a weird caddy car with a built in seat where you put the clubs into the bag head first and the handles stood proud. I think he had a clear plastic cover to put over the when it rained which it usually did. He was a bit part-actor and appeared in the Irvine Welsh film Acid House. He also played Stan

in the Rab C Nesbitt TV series, Priest in The Book Group and a hangman in Martin Scorsese's film Gangs of New York.

We once played 9 holes together so that is my only claim to fame. He was very polite and a steady player, but I don't know how he managed to keep his white shoes clean on the muddy course.

He was also a stand- up comic but latterly his act was very blue and politically incorrect and he died suddenly in 2015. See the web for some of his jokes.

Ronnie Simpson

The Lisbon Lion - what a true gent. Ronnie Simpson was the veteran footballer who played for Celtic when they won the European Cup in 1967 - the first UK side to triumph in that event. He was also famous for his goalkeeping feats - when at Hibs in 1961-1962 he saved seven consecutive penalties.

I partnered him at a police golf outing at Leven Thistle in the mid-1990s when he was on the Pools Panel. He was quite small by modern-day goalkeeping standards and was very pleasant, modest man. Although a bit out of practice he soon got into his stride, and as we turned into the wind he hit long, low booming drives with a touch of draw. He talked of playing golf at Foxton Hall, Alnmouth when he and his family had a caravan there when he played for Newcastle United. By current standards he never made a lot of money out of football - Celtic were always notoriously mean at paying players. When he retired, he ran a sports shop in Rose Street in Edinburgh for a while until it folded, then he became a pub landlord. He said he had a nice house in Barnton in Edinburgh, a lovely family and he turned up in an old Ford Fiesta. He said he was not envious of the rewards players took from the game nowadays.

Ray McIlwraith

I met his son years later as he was a reporter with the Daily Record and covered court cases.

He was a tidy golfer off about 11 and played at Baberton. Ray would be in his 50's when I played him in the Hydro Board summer knock out cup. I was warned not to play him at Baberton where he was almost unbeatable but to take him to Silverknowes and unsettle him with the vandalised greens and parties of intruders who walked across the course from the Muirhouse scheme towards the beach at Cramond as if they owned the place. The kids might steal your ball or make V signs at you.

I was also warned about Ray's unusual golf swing. Sure enough as billed he took a couple of conventional practice swings, but when he played his shot his body bent double at the waist on the follow through. Far from keeping his head steady it dropped about two feet from his position at address. Somehow, by dint of getting about 12 strokes from the great man, I was still in touch at the idiosyncratic sixteenth which required a right angled right to left tee shot, then won the seventeenth where the bunkers were used as children's slides. By the time we played the 601 yard uphill, side hill eighteenth into the prevailing wind, he was tired out and his swing faltered. It was one of my few famous victories.

Sir Douglas Haddow.

After Sir Douglas retired as head of the Civil Service in Scotland he became chairman of the Hydro-Electric Board. With the help of his kindly but fierce looking Secretary (think Rosa Klebb) he organised the Hydro Board golf section with outings and competitions. In the foursomes we put our names in and a draw was made so that we would partner someone from another part of Head Office, where engineers, surveyors, wayleave officers and people from the commercial department worked as well as us lawyers.

Sir Douglas was a competitive man; that was probably how he got to the top, and somehow he was always partnered by fellow Bruntsfield member Wilson Imrie from the Commercial team who was rock solid off 10 to Sir Douglas's slightly erratic 12. I was partnered by Bill Jones, an Englishman on the engineering side, who was very sporty, had just given up rugby and had taken to golf late with the extra enthusiasm such sporting folk possess.

Bill was already a better golfer than me in my mid-twenties - although a 15 year veteran of the sport. He teed off at the first and sliced the ball into a coppice of staked trees. Had I known the rules better I could have had a free drop two club lengths way from the offending object. Sir Douglas and Wilson remained quiet, within the Rules of Golf and did not offer any assistance. Despite being in the rough I took out my trusty 4 iron and made quite a good swing on the ball but did not realise I had followed through on to the tree and my dear old pre-war fake wood steel shaft melted round the tree while under tension and snapped. I repeated the same feat with a Mizuno 4 iron about 25 years later, feeling no impact on either occasion.

As a result we were always under the cosh playing Sir Douglas and his partner. However at the ninth, by which time we must have been about four down, the normally consistent Wilson put Sir Douglas in a bunker. Did I say that Sir Douglas in his 60s played in a Boy Scout cap, long shorts and long socks with flashes on his garters? It was an accepted look in those innocent times; nowadays you would probably get arrested. Anyway, Sir Douglas entered this fairly deep bunker and took a huge amount of sand but managed to get the ball out just and it landed perched on top of the bunker in the fringe a yard or so from the putting surface. "Oh well out, Sir Douglas!" shouted my playing partner in mock acclamation. Sir Douglas was furious and said nothing but his flushed face told all. The normally expressionless Wilson permitted a sly smile and we won that hole although we had to shake hands some way from home having been well beaten.

It was nevertheless a great opportunity to meet these great men, and it helped a bit when I had some work to hand in to Sir Douglas's Office or to assist the Commercial Department.

'DJ'

DJ Johnson was a work colleague at the Hydro-Electric Board. He and Barty Braithwaite were both in their 60s and while very experienced were otherwise unemployable and my boss James Aitken in the Conveyancing Department was always chasing them up about some land transactions they had outstanding. By contrast my room-mate, the industrious David Elder and future brother-in-law Douglas Purdom kept me on the straight and narrow.

DJ was also a member at Bruntsfield, though played infrequently, but realising my modest golfing skills offered to take me for a mid- week evening round in the summer. I was warned beforehand by Barty that DJ liked the odd mulligan as he was very much a 24 handicap man, though apparently had been a decent golfer in his youth. DJ was quite tall, balding with a flaky head and smoked a bent Sherlock Holmes-type pipe incessantly, although most of the time was spent relighting or refilling the bowl. It soon became obvious his golfing skills were limited and rusty and I was quite happy, being a non-competitive sort of chap, that we would not bother keeping scores or indeed holes won or lost. DJ would hack his way about until he got within 100 yards of the hole where he seemed to wake up and try to hit a high, floating pitch shot to the green. If he duffed this shot he would mutter "I'll just have another go if you don't mind" and immediately dropped another ball from his pocket, and delivered a second blow which as often as not landed on the green. He prided himself in this part of his game and seemed quite happy to pitch a few close in an otherwise indifferent round. It was a lovely evening and although Bruntsfield was far too posh a club for me, I marvelled at is design whereby each hole was at a different angle to the wind as you turned around the trees, and it had a bit of topography to test all your shots.

After some indifferent school qualifications and an ordinary degree, I soon prospered in the office setting with all of these characters like Les the Magician who used to sneak off from work in his Morris Minor to do childrens' parties complete with white rabbit in a cage. Mike Brogan introduced me to the 6 pint lunch which I never tried again as I soon fell asleep in the afternoon at my desk, and had a hangover by 8 pm when I was supposed to go out with my fiancée! I am not saying golf helped me get up the corporate ladder in any way, but I came to appreciate my colleagues and after the narrow age band of school and University colleagues enjoyed working with men and women of all ages from 16 to 65. The older men were retiring and occasionally would tell war tales or speak with pride about being at the Hydro Board when it was founded by Tom Johnston during the Second World War. It brought power to the glens at the same time as the introduction of the NHS and other radical changes in an age when austerity was a virtue borne lightly due to hope for a better future. There is nothing like an office or works golf outing to improve morale.

Alan Finlayson

Alan was like a father to me although I had a wonderful Dad. I met him in the 1980s when we were both members of the Lothian Region Child Protection Committee. He looked after cases involving children and I dealt with adult criminal cases. We met regularly and always had a good chat. He came from Dumfries, and as a Doonhamer was a life-long Queen of the South football fan and long suffering member of the Tartan Army but old enough to remember when Scotland men qualified for the World Cup. He was a small burly, cheery man with glasses and when he took early retirement to work on projects to do with child law reform he was appointed a Temporary Sheriff. He could not drive himself, but through a combination of public transport and the driving skills of his long-suffering wife Dorothy, he managed to sit in all 50 of the Courts in Scotland. These varied from the big city ones in Edinburgh and Glasgow to the picturesque ones at Lochmaddy in North Uist, Dornoch, Stornoway and Lerwick in Shetland. On account of his appearance he was known as Rumpole, and although his health was a bit precarious at times, he was always cheery, popular and kind to young people setting out in a career. He had angina in his legs and managed to find fairly bland black trainers to wear on the bench and at other times to ease his feet. He doctor told him to cut his drinking to 4 units a day but every now and again he would open the pub at home at 11 50 pm and have 4 decent drinks in the next half hour!

He was also a member at Bruntsfield and in the 1980s and 90s took me there for a few evening rounds. Being a sporty type of person, who also loved cricket, and although about 20 years older than me, he could still hit a few decent shots, and usually as we reached the sixteenth Alan would be a hole or two ahead. I didn't panic though because I knew his legs would begin to tire as we made our way uphill to towards the clubhouse. With a bit of luck I might win the seventeenth and eighteenth to win or tie the game.

Dave Crown

My cousin Gordon has lived and worked in Spain for over 20 years and now and again I visit him near La Manga in the bottom South East corner of Spain where he lives.

On one visit I had my golf clubs with me, but Gordon was too busy at work to play, so fixed up a game with his friend Dave who used to play professional football for Brentford, Reading Exeter City, Gillingham and Southend United. He sensibly qualified as an accountant when he was still playing so the transition to civvy life after he retired from the game was less challenging than many of his contemporaries. It was boom time in the mid-2000s, and the Brits had bought up many flats on the Costa Blanca taking over from the Germans who pulled out largely on account of the second home tax imposed to help pay for German re-unification. Dave was semi-retired, and split his time between Blighty and La Manga, but was able to continue working as an accountant doing the books for sole traders on line and helping them with their tax affairs. Gordon fixed us up at a course near Murcia and we set off in my hire car on a fine day. By the time we got there all buggies had been taken and we set off in the heat with caddy cars and plenty bottles of water. I had a new hot Taylor Made driver which was working well and I was soon in the lead. As time passed Dave's fitness began to kick in but worse was to follow. I was wearing swimming shorts and after a while the lining began to chaff my tender parts. That is my excuse - how else could I lose the game when four up with five to play! We set off for home but

I noticed we were low on diesel fuel and there were no filling stations on the motorway. Eventually the car ground to a halt. We were in the middle of nowhere but scrambled across a field to a pub where we explained our predicament in pidgin Spanish, and organised a taxi. It arrived at the pub but with a plastic bag of petrol so we had to travel back to the filling station to buy diesel then set off for the car. Our mobile phones had run out of charge and it was almost search party time when we arrived home sometime after midnight.

I was too polite to say to Dave why my game had deteriorated and complimented him on his never-say-die attitude honed from his years as a professional footballer. Needless to say when I confided in Gordon he had great delight telling Dave the full story. I can't wait to have a return match sometime in cooler climes!

Danny

When I started buying and selling golf clubs seriously in the late 1990's, I met Chris Boyle, the cheery owner of a second hand shop in Stockbridge. He was a member at Liberton on the South side of Edinburgh, which is a picturesque track with fine views to the South and East of Edinburgh. Although on the short side it was still problematic for me. Chris had been a butcher to trade and had very strong wrists and forearms through years of chopping meat, and although a few years older than me was still very fit and could hit the ball for miles, albeit not always in the right direction. Sometimes a dark haired man called Danny would help out in the shop in the background but was a man of few words.

Danny had a difficult upbringing, fragile mental health and I understood a bit of a drink problem though I never experienced it at first hand. He had been champion golfer at Liberton off 1 I think, and now played off 6 but was very steady. He was keen to play longer, more challenging courses, but we started with the municipal courses of Edinburgh, including Silverknowes, Carricknowe, Craigentinny, Portobello and the magnificent Braid Hills. We then broadened our horizons with outings to Magdalene Fields and Goswick, near Berwick upon Tweed, Eyemouth and even Southerness, that wonderful Dumfriesshire links. On good days I could win a few holes but Danny didn't mind my clumsiness. He was a slight man, with black hair slicked back in an old fashioned style, and while not a long hitter was steady and straight, reaching about 220 to 240 yards off the tee, usually down the middle. If I was upsides of Danny, the chances were his second shot was much better than mine and his short game was where he excelled.

We talked about golf, football and horse racing as we played. Danny would occasionally speak about the darts league he was in at the golf club, although this dried up after some sort of incident when he was banned for a spell. He still stayed at home with his parents, and apart from a short spell as a settler in a bookmaker's shop did not seem capable of holding down a steady job.

Eventually he a had a nervous breakdown and I visited him a few times in hospital but on his release he did not want to play golf anymore and then did not return my calls. Chris did say Danny would acquire and drop friends. I do miss his undemanding friendship, beautifully controlled swing and modesty about his golfing achievements which he often put down to good luck. In his presence I played some of my best golf.

These are some of the characters who have livened up my game. I have made many friendships on the golf course, where it can become competitive like the gladiators of the tennis arenas, but there is more to it than that especially if the weather turns bad. And when locked in battle, and you have to (appear to) earnestly search for your opponent's ball or hold the flag while your opponent putts. Over time you appreciate your opponent's game or look away if it upsets you. If they resort to gamesmanship you know you have the edge. Once I was warned ahead of a mixed foursomes tie that my male opponent was legendary for claiming his putt was nearer the hole, forcing you to putt first. Sure enough he tried that stunt after a few holes, and I stepped up and managed to sink my one. He was flustered by this and mystified, but I did not challenge his assertion. We did manage to beat this doughty opponent but enjoyed a nice drink in the bar afterwards and genuine good wishes for the next round.

That is why golf is unique, and while playing alone with two golf balls is fun and ensures personal honesty, playing with others is what it is all about.

My Final Rant

Golf is a wonderful game; yet why are we playing less of it and allowing golf courses to close? There are lots of reasons, and all sorts of committees have looked into the problem and usually come up with the solution - getting club members to pay more money.

I remember as a young man starting out at work, where my boss encouraged me to join the office curling team. In those days we went to the old Haymarket Rink in Edinburgh for a mid- week evening game and the place was packed with middle-aged men whose wives, if they had them, were golf widows in the summer and curling widows in the winter.

Recently my son learned to play curling at school, and when I picked him up at the Murrayfield Ice rink (next to the famous rugby stadium) I was shocked to see how few people were going out to play the 5 30 pm games. Most games are now played during the day by retired men and women.

There have been social changes and not everyone can escape from family for a half or a whole day to play golf. Peter McEvoy, legendary amateur golfer and course designer devised PowerPlay golf over 9 holes where you play to the flag that is best for you, then total up the points. He also designed a course which was split into three six hole sections, each of which could be played in an hour. Many courses nowadays are split into two nines, enabling golfers to play shorter rounds if they wish, allowing more players to start at once.

Sadly some courses have issues in allowing play to start from other than the first tee, which negates the value of this type of course design. Professional golf has made the game slower and seduced us all into embarking with a full set of 14 clubs whereas a set of 7 in a pencil bag will do most of us most of the time.

It was heartening to see Tiger Woods win the 2019 Masters after some years in the wilderness, and hopefully his victory will encourage others to play. However, don't turn up in that red turtle neck number he wore on the last day, as you won't be allowed to play at many clubs unless your shirt has a collar. Don't wear jeans either; older members have not quite got Elvis's blue jeans out of their heads. In 1954 they were poised to destroy the very fabric of society. I once got told off for wearing short shorts and short socks and some other dress transgression I fail to recall. To be fair to the R & A and their Rules, clothes standards are not mentioned. All you need to do is wear something that will not obviously cause offence to others. Why can't you wear trainers? Most modern golf shoes look like them anyway. Why can top amateurs wear shorts but not male professionals?   I'm pleased to say that's just changed for practice rounds and pro-ams, but it was a long time coming. I would draw the line at the unbridled use of mobile phones while playing, and I'm still not sure about the apparel marketed and worn by John Daly.

The one huge advantage golf has over most other sports is through the handicapping system. Provided you get down to a low handicap (scratch) you can enter the Open. Since 2005, suitably qualified female golfers can also enter, although none have to date. More recently a mixed professional tournament was played, and women regularly compete in the British Par 3 championship at Nailcote Hall off the same tees as the men. A few more tournaments like that might percolate down to club level. What about more mixed medals with women getting to play off shorter tees to make things more interesting? Most men don't fancy the idea of being beaten by lassies but I am sure we could all get used to the idea.

So there you have it. Shorter courses with fewer holes, less clubs and clutter and wear what you want. If you see me competing in a mixed tournament in a three piece suit with a starched collar and a tie, and carrying an ancient pencil bag of cleeks, it is just my idea of fun!

Glossary

Item	Description	Referred in (see code explanation at end of Glossary)
Argent Brierley	Described in the book as relating to Rod Argent, leader of the rock band 'The Zombies'. In reality, Brierley was an artist, first seen by the author as the signatory to a painting of Cramond dated 1911. His biography states 'Landscape painter and teacher in Worcester, William Argent Brierley (1893 – 1960), who after attending George Heriot's School in Edinburgh gained his diploma at Edinburgh College of Art'.	TBC
avizandum	A Scots law term. Where a judge takes time to consider their judgment	TD
Beldam Lascar Packing	Refers to a very much defunct (but still present) shop at 7 Queen Charlotte Street, Leith. In 1876, Marine Engineer Asplan Beldam invented a seal ('Packing') to stop the steam escaping on ships, in order to allow them to go faster. He went on to form Beldam Packing and Rubber Company, and continued to create and market many more inventions. Lascar derives from the Arabic '*Al-Ashkar*' meaning Sailor from East India, but the term was used as	PGNW

Item	Description	Referred in (see code explanation at end of Glossary)
	shorthand for any non-European serving on a British vessel. The Beldam group had branches and agents in many ports throughout the World, and this was just another albeit small outlet. The business survives to this day as Beldam Crossley.	
Bunnet	An old Scots word - A style of flat cap traditionally made from wool, commonly worn by farmers and country gentlemen in cool climates	CE TBC TTM TD PGNW
Cleek	1829 – An iron headed club with a straight narrow face and long shaft. A bit like a modern day putter, or perhaps a jigger (1893 – a short iron headed club used for 'approaching')	TTM PGNW MFGB
Eisenhower tree	A description for any large, golf-awkwardly placed tree on a golf course. The iconic Eisenhower Tree once stood on the 17th hole at Augusta National. The native loblolly pine was more than 80 years old and 65 feet high when it suffered extensive damage from a major ice storm and had to be removed in February 2014. The tree gained its name in the 1950's when then-U.S. President Dwight D. Eisenhower, an Augusta National member from 1948 until his death in 1969, unsuccessfully lobbied to have it taken down after it interfered with his tee shot in 1956. Chairman Clifford Roberts ruled him out of order.	CE
ex tempore	A legal term that means 'at the time'. A judge who hands down a decision in a case soon or straight after hearing it is delivering a decision ex tempore	TD

Item	Description	Referred in (see code explanation at end of Glossary)
Feathery balls a.k.a. Featheries	Originated in 1724 in Scotland, possibly earlier elsewhere. Formed from a leather pouch stuffed with bird feathers. Gutties (q.v.) started to replace them from 1848	Info. entry only
Florin	1849 – 1967. A UK currency coin worth two shillings until decimalisation in 1971 when is became a 10p piece. It was demonetised on 30 June 1993	MFGB
Foursomes	1867 A match in which four players take part, two against two, the partners on each side playing alternately, each side playing one ball. All players drive on odd and even holes. The format is used in match and stroke play.	Several refs.
Gate putting style	That little known golfer, Tiger Woods, describes his gate putting routine thus: "I use this drill all the time. Three feet from a hole, I push two tees in the ground just outside the heel and toe, forming a gate for the putter head, then ensure the club passes through the gate when committing to the putting stroke".	CE
Gutty balls a.k.a. Gutties	1890 – Golfers' slang for Gutta Percha golf balls. These originated in 1848, but by 1860 were generally being used rather than 'featheries'. Gutta Percha is dried gum resin from guttiferous trees, especially the Malaysian sapodilla. It has a rubber-like feel and is formed into ball shapes by heating it up and shaping it while hot. Balls which fracture and break can be reformed, painted and reused.	PGNW MFGB

Item	Description	Referred in (see code explanation at end of Glossary)
Haskell balls	1899, but replaced Gutty balls from around 1920. They were formed of a solid core wrapped tightly with rubber threads, and covered with a layer of Gutta Percha. Although the first two piece balls were developed in 1902, it would be the mid 1960's when the Haskell covers were replaced with a durable plastic. Two and three piece balls proliferated thereafter.	PGNW MFGB
Hickory clubs	Refers to the wood used for the shafts. The heads were made of beech or fruiting trees, and most clubs had wooden heads until the introduction of gutty balls, as metal heads tended to damage the softer feathery balls. Hickory club use, and competitions have become popular in recent years.	TTM PGNW TGCOH MFGB
Honourable Company of Edinburgh Golfers (HCEG)	Also known as 'Muirfield' due to the course where HCEG members play. Members are usually distinguished pillars of society, and exclusively male until 2017. Played on Leith Links from 1744 until 1836, then Musselburgh until 1891 when they moved to the rarefied atmosphere at the East end of Gullane.	TBC PGNW
Hosel	The hosel is the component of a golf club where the shaft is connected to the clubhead. Typically, the hosel is part of the clubhead, and the shaft slides into the hosel and is secured with glue, which nowadays is usually an epoxy.	Info entry only
Jigger	1893 – A short iron headed club used for 'approaching' (presumably short shots to the green). Some controversy has surrounded this club in recent years, mainly its legality in the USA. Frequently found in golf bags of HCEG members.	PGNW

Item	Description	Referred in (see code explanation at end of Glossary)
Links	The ground on which golf is played - more or less level or gently undulating sandy ground near the sea-shore, covered with turf, coarse grass etc (this definition from the Shorter Oxford Dictionary). The word *links* comes via the Scots language from the Old English word *hlinc* meaning *rising ground or ridge*, and refers to an area of coastal sand dunes and sometimes to open parkland. In practice, Links land consisted of sandy substrate which was unsuitable for agriculture, and barely even useful for sheep grazing, so the advent of golf gave it a useful purpose. Some think that the origin of *Links* is the Dutch (and German) word for *Left*, which used to have bad connotations, and even relate to the Devil – thus unmanageable ground could be seen as worse than useless. Just as well golf came along to save the day!	TBC TTM TD MGR PGBW WIAA TCGOH
Linksy	Pertaining to conditions on Links golf courses. Due to hard, running fairways and frequent wind, the golf ball should be kept low, both to take advantage of the fairway run, and to avoid interference from head winds	PGNW
Major(s)	The four most important golf tournaments in the World calendar. The Masters, The US PGA, the US Open and The Open. With the exception of the Masters which is always played at Augusta in Atlanta Georgia USA, the others rotate annually, the Open in the United Kingdom, and the US PGA and US Open in the USA.	TBC

Item	Description	Referred in (see code explanation at end of Glossary)
Mashie, Mashie Niblick	See Niblick	Info entry only
Maurice Flitcroft 'scandal'	Flitcroft was a virtual beginner, never having completed 18 holes on a proper golf course, when he entered for the 1976 Open and took 121 strokes for the round, comfortably the highest score in the Open's history. He entered a further seven but made it to only two, in 1984 and 1990, using false names – 'Gerald Hoppy' and 'Paychecki' before being outed by R&A officials. He died in 2007.	CE
Mills-type putter	The TP Mills Klassic was originally a design made for Tommy Armour III and was used to set what was at the time the PGA All Time Record Low Score of 254. The design features a rounded toe and parallel pocket. David Mills, TP Mills' son, reputedly examines every single putter that leaves the TP Mills Co. shop	MFGB
Mulligan	A Mulligan is a second chance to perform an action, usually after the first chance has gone wrong through bad luck or a blunder. Its best-known meaning is in golf, where a player is informally allowed to replay a stroke, even though this is against the formal rules of the game. The Mulligan is usually permitted only on the first tee, but some golfers use one Mulligan per nine holes. This convention is sometimes also referred to as a 'bisque'. It's most common for Mulligans to be used only off the tee, but some groups also allow Mulligans from the fairway.	CIHMOGC

Item	Description	Referred in (see code explanation at end of Glossary)
	The term is allegedly named after Canadian-born amateur David Bernard Mulligan who had established himself as a prominent member of clubs that included Winged Foot. In the late 1920s, Mulligan had a regular club foursome, which he often drove to the course in a 1920s vintage Briscoe, a touring car. Once on the first tee, the story goes, his partners allowed him to hit a second ball after mishitting his drive. Mulligan complained that his hands were still numb after driving rough roads. The other three looked at him with considerable puzzlement, and one of them asked, "What are you doing?" "I'm taking a correction shot,' he replied." His playing partner asked what he called that. Thinking fast, and on the spur of the moment, he told him that he called it a 'Mulligan.' And so the legend was born (unless you believe the claim that John A. 'Buddy' Mulligan, a locker room attendant in the 1930s at Essex Fells Country Club, New .Jersey had a similar set of circumstances...)	
Niblick	An iron with a heavy, lofted head, similar to a modern day nine-iron, used especially for playing out of bunkers. A *Mashie* Niblick is a club with an iron head, the face having more slope than a mashie iron but less slope than a mashie niblick. In modern day numbering, a mashie would equate (approximately) to a five iron, a mashie niblick to a seven, and a niblick to a nine. These names have origins between 1862 and 1881	Info entry only

Item	Description	Referred in (see code explanation at end of Glossary)
Open (or *The* Open)	Not the *British* Open, just 'The Open'. Comfortably the oldest of the four Majors, first held in 1860 compared to the US Open first held in 1895	CE
Pencil bag	A lightweight golf bag intended to carry just a few clubs. Mainly for summer use.	MFR
Pools Panel	Football matches forming part of a Pools draw, would, if matches were postponed, often have their results adjudicated for the sake of the football pools results, by a board known as the Pools Panel. It was formed in 1963 when a particularly cold winter scrapped football for three weeks running. It still operates to this day, the current Board consisting of just two members, Geoff Hunt and Tony Green. Gordon Banks was the third member until his death in February 2019.	CIHMOGC
Proof	In a legal context, this refers simply to a hearing where evidence from witnesses is heard. The Court will expect to hold a full hearing at which all issues in the case can be dealt with. That is often referred to as a 'proof'. It is the stage when the parties get an opportunity to prove their case.	TD
R&A	The Royal and Ancient Golf Club of St Andrews. Established in 1754, it is the third oldest Golf Club (or Society) in the World (after Royal Burgess and HCEG). The R&A is the ruling authority of golf throughout the world except in North America. First admitted Lady members in February 2015.	MFR

Item	Description	Referred in (see code explanation at end of Glossary)
Segue	Refers to the connection between golf club shaft and the head - an uninterrupted transition from one piece to the other	CE
Schenectady putter	In the early 1900s, center-shafted, mallet-headed putters, such as the Schenectady model, were becoming increasingly popular in the United States. In 1910, The R&A added two new Decisions on the Rules of Golf that spoke to croquet mallets specifically and deemed 'the various mallet-headed implements' to no longer be permissible for use. However, the USGA interpreted 'mallet-headed' differently and continued to allow putters like the Schenectady and Hackbarth models to be used in the United States. This difference in interpretation between The R&A and the USGA was rectified in 1952, when both organizations came together to jointly release the first uniform code of the Rules of Golf to be used worldwide. At this time, it was decided that the putter shaft could be fixed to the putter head at any point, which permitted the Schenectady putter, and other similar styles, to be used anywhere in the world. The Hackbarth model mentioned above, however, is no longer permitted because of the way the shaft connects to the clubhead.	MFGB
Shrieval	Of or relating to a Sheriff (1681)	INTRO

Item	Description	Referred in (see code explanation at end of Glossary)
Silverfield	A fictional golf club in Edinburgh. Readers may notice similarities to Murrayfield, with touches of Silverknowes and Mortonhall	Most entries
Skoosh	Scottish. Means 'squirt', but also 'easy'	TBC
Spoon (also Tour Spoon)	Originally (1808) 'A wooden golf club having a slightly concave head'. Modern examples often equate to a 5 wood, but the Taylor Made Tour Spoon was generally 13° loft, making it equivalent to a 3 wood.	CE TBC MFGB
Ping Square Grooves controversy	There was a specific technical issue with Ping Eye 2 clubs made between 1985 and 1989, as determined by the US PGA. The issue was not 'square grooves' per se, but whether the grooves on these clubs were .005" too closely spaced (that's the thickness of a human hair). Following extensive lawsuits, the PGA eventually dropped its opposition to square grooves in 1993	CE
Scottish Boys Amateur Golf Championship	Inaugurated 1935. Past winners include such luminaries as Ronnie Shade and Andrew Coltart, while more recent winners who are competing on the European Tour include millennials Scott Henry, David Law, Grant Forrest, Bradley Neil and Ewen Ferguson.	TBC
Stymie	Golf isn't a sport where in the present era you can play defence against your opponent, but once you could. For many years in singles match play, a person wasn't allowed to move his or her ball on the green even if it was directly in an opponent's path.	MFGB

Item	Description	Referred in (see code explanation at end of Glossary)
	A player facing the obstacle while trying to hole out was known as being 'stymied.' They could either try to putt around an opponent's ball or putt or chip over it. There were revisions to this rule over the years before it was totally abolished worldwide in 1952.	
Tonneau cover	A tonneau covers is used to protect unoccupied passenger seats in a convertible and roadster vehicles.	TTM
TP Mills	TP Mills was a master putter/designer and his initials graced a number of putters over the years as well as made to measure ones from his own should he designed for Wilson, Mizuno, Slazenger, and currently Taylor Made. He is credited with many advances in putter design, including making the putter head black, thus offering a greater contrast between the ball and the putter; marking the true sweet spot; marking his name on the face of the putter; sweeping the weight towards the putter toe; and designing the 'slant heel' located behind the hosel. Many of these characteristics have since become standard in the golf industry.	TGCOH
Trap (also sand-trap)	The USA equivalent of a bunker. Our Transatlantic cousins do have a habit of, some might say, unnecessarily changing perfectly good English terms, and this is an example. Perhaps not as bad as their conversion of the perfectly satisfactory and logical progression of *albatross* (three under par) to the unattractive and overly complicated *double-eagle*.	CE TTM

Item	Description	Referred in (see code explanation at end of Glossary)
Vardon grip	The Vardon grip, or overlapping grip, is the grip most prevalent among professional golfers. In the Vardon grip, one places the little finger of the trailing hand (the one placed lower on the club – right hand for a right-handed player) in between the index and middle finger on the leading hand (the hand that is higher on the club). The leading-hand thumb should fit in the lifeline of the trailing hand. Vardon actually took up this grip some time after Johnny Laidlay, a champion Scottish amateur player, invented it.	MFGB
Whin	A pesky shrub, proliferates on golf courses. Not a golfer's friend. From Middle English *whynne*, from Old Norse *hvein* ("gorse, furze")	CE PGNW
Window (wartime countermeasure)	**Window,** laterally called **Chaff** by the British and *Düppel* by the Second World War era German Luftwaffe (from the Berlin suburb where it was first developed), is a radar countermeasure in which aircraft or other targets spread a cloud of small, thin pieces of aluminium, metallized glass fibre or plastic, which either appears as a cluster of primary targets on radar screens or swamps the screen with multiple returns.	PGNW

Referred In

CE – Close Encounter
CIHMOGC – Characters I have met on the golf course
HTFYS – How to fix your slice
INTRO - Introduction
MFGB – My Favourite Golf Books
MFR – My Final Rant
MGR – My golfing romance
PGNW – Play Golf, not War
TBC – The Boys' Champion
TD – The Deal
TGCOH – The Golf Club O-Holic
TTM – The Thirties man
WIAA – Was it an Ace?

Photographs and memorabilia

The book is liberally sprinkled with references to photographs and memorabilia. The following are a few examples which haven't manged to be fitted in elsewhere....

Malcolm (Moly) McMillan, Gordon Samson, The Author and Brian Fearon on the Apex Senior Tour outing to Mortonhall GC, Edinburgh, September 2018

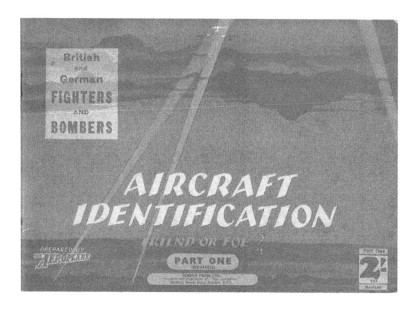

WWII Aircraft Identification booklet. Mentioned in
'Play Golf not War'

Frank's trophy room after 50 years... Crown Office pro-am,
Handicap prize bowl made by Brian Brown, and a bent wee cup
purchased for £2, retained by Frank

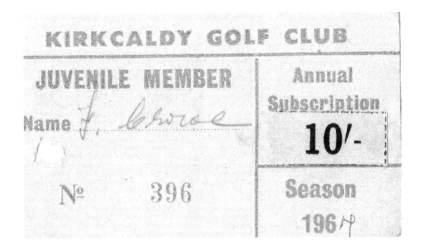

The Author's first Golf Club membership – to the
Balwearie Club in Kirkcaldy in 1964

Frank with Smudge and Bella

264

Moly, Frank and Fran at Ashludie GC, 14th June 2019

Silverfield Layout and Scorecard

Silverfield is a fictitious course, blended mainly from Murrayfield and Silverknowes layouts. It is perhaps the only course in the World to have twenty three holes.

Silverfield Golf Club scorecard
'The World's only 23 hole golf course'

Score	Hole No.	Name	Yds	Yds	Par	Stroke index	Yds	Par	Stroke index
	1	Good game	383	375	4	5		5	13
	2	Hit and Hope	132	124	3	17		3	22
	3	R.A.B.T	419	411	4	1		5	3
	4	All Downhill	360	353	4	13		4	9
	5	Blind Shot	333	325	4	3		4	1
	6	Handshake	310	304	4	7		4	7
	7	Lost Ball	186	163	3	11		3	20
	8	Crown & Plate	315	310	4	15		4	5
	9	Henkel	262	252	4	9		4	11
	10	Alien's Reach	194	164	3	6		3	19
	11	Cherry Trees	393	387	4	2		4	2
	12	Golden Barries	306	322	4	18		4	21
			3715	3533	45		3242	47	

Score	Hole No.	Name	Yds	Yds	Par	Stroke index	Yds	Par	Stroke index
	13	Fate it in	127	122	3	16		3	16
	14	Eisenhower	507	484	5	6		5	6
	15	Keep Left	349	346	4	14		4	2
	16	Gently Does it	353	350	4	8		4	4
	17	White Squirrel	327	312	4	15		4	12
	18	Duke's Repose	525	462	5	12		5	14
	19	Not the 19th	369	361	4	18		4	10
	20	Commodore	155	150	3	23		3	17
	21	Hooker's Heaven	448	446	4	4		5	4
	22	Happy Howdah	208	283	4	17		4	14
	23	Bevvies in	601	596	5	10		5	6
			4049	3912	45		3705	46	

	Yds	Yds	Par		Yds	Par
IN	3715	3533	45		3242	47
OUT	4049	3912	45		3705	46
TOTAL	7764	7445	90		6947	93

Handicap ☐

Net Score ☐   Stableford Points ☐

Marker's Signature ....

Player's signature ....

Book Characters

The editor noticed early in the publishing process that the Author had provided careful and comprehensive details of a characters in the stories. These are a few along with the accompanying text from the stories.

The Duke (Ruaridh Morrison)
He was likened to the Duke of Windsor circa 1937. He was resplendent in plus 4's, tweed jacket, check shirt, cravat, brown brogues topped with a smart bunnet of the type sported by trainers of National Hunt racehorses. He always arrived in a beautiful 1930's supercharged sports car called a Squire which was maroon with black wings and very rakish, no windscreen, just a couple of aero screens

Ms Jenny Hinton
This description circa 2000. She was about 5' 7" of medium build,
clearly sporty and smartly but fashionably dressed in a matching
green outfit of a skirt and top and pushing an electric trolley filled
with new, shiny Taylor Made clubs

Deimos
He carried a silver pencil bag containing bronze coloured irons.
As he walked away, I saw a mark down the side of his neck, about
6 inches long, like a gill, but it was just a flash. I noticed he was
wearing golf gloves on each hand.   His hair was peculiar, but I
only got a flash of it

Jimmy Gibb (as an 18 year old)

The locker room door crashed open and it came this tall guy with an ancient worn leather pencil bag slung over his right shoulder and a Tennant's lager plastic carrier bag in his other hand which seemed to contain a few bits and pieces. He had spiky hair, a scar down his left cheek and was wearing black drainpipes trousers, black suede brothel creeper shoes and a double breasted black cowboy-type shirt which had white piping on the front and cuffs. He took off his shoes revealing day-glo socks and proceeded to put on a plain pair of black golf shoes which had "kilties", fringed tongues covering the laces.

The assembled characters in the book

Aside the four main characters depicted on the previous page, there are a further three which have been assembled into a photomontage, making seven in all (the book title page includes just five, the Author accompanied by the main four characters).

The splendid artwork, by professional illustrator Rob Anderson, has brought these characters to life.

The characters, from left to right, are as follows.

Happy Howden	He was a regular face at on the golf course and stood out with his bald head, white cap, immaculate golf clothes and pristine white shoes. He was a bit part-actor and appeared in the Irvine Welsh film Acid House. He also played Stan in the Rab C Nesbitt TV series, Priest in The Book Group and a hangman in Martin Scorsese's film Gangs of New York.
The Duke	Real name Ruaridh Morrison, was resplendent in plus 4's, tweed jacket, check shirt, cravat and brown brogues, topped with a smart bunnet of the type sported by trainers of National Hunt racehorses.
Deimos	Features in 'Close Encounters'. Secrecy prevents further disclosure…
The Author (as Argent Brierley)	Brierley is famed as an Open Champion in 'The Boy's Champion', but pobably is the Author's alter ego.
Jimmy Gibb	First seen as an 18 year old in 'The Boys Champion', and reappears many years later in the same story.
Jennie Hinton	First encountered by the Author early in 'My Golfing Romance' and while their relationship was not initially converted into marriage, it was by the end of the tale.
Old Budgie, the fruit machine barfly	Old Budgie at the club (Balwearie) who poured a small fortune into the one armed bandit most weekends, but as far as is known never experienced the noise of coins pouring out in a jackpot pay-out – that much advertised promise on the side of the machine. He is however shown here enjoying his modest winnings.

What's in the Author's bag?

The Author frequently refers to golf clubs both in fiction and non-fiction entries. Given that he claims to have owned over forty sets of clubs, one hundred putters and a vast assortment of other golfing paraphernalia, it's perhaps surprising that he manages to restrict himself to fourteen clubs. This is however his claim, and the following appears to be the current favourites. We've also featured Jimmy Gibb's bag from his 1990's Scottish Boy's Championship win.

Ping G400 10.5 degree driver
Ping G30 3 wood 13 degrees, 5 wood 18 degrees + 22 degree rescue
Ping Crossover 4 iron
Benross Compressor irons 5- PW
Ping Zing Sand and Lob Wedges
Ping nickel J blade.

Frank's bag, Saturday 11th May 2019

Maruman Conductor 31CXII 1 - PW irons,
Taylor Made Tour 55 degrees sand wedge,
Ping Eye Nos 1 & 3 woods
Ping Anser putter

**Jimmy Gibb's Bag,
Circa 1990**
(The Clubs with which
he won the Scottish
Boys Championship)

....and while we're here, some of Author's other putters shown on the right are...
Grasshopper Chipper/Jigger
David Low No 9 putter with punch dot face
St Andrews Gem muscle bag putter of the type used by
Bobby Locke
Bowyer's Bee-Line
Schenectady–style
putter
Mill's aluminium
headed   putter
about 1935
Titleist Bull's Eye
Ping's first putter

Golf Clubs featuring in the Book.

This book would not be complete without some photographic examples of the clubs quoted in both fiction and non-fiction entries.

Taylor Made Tour Spoon. Jock used it to fade a shot past the Eisenhower Tree on the 14th at Silverfield in 'Close Encounter'

Wilson TPA XVIII Putter: The Hon. John's putter in 'The Deal'

A Honma 7 Iron. These Japanese Clubs, favoured by the rich and famous, were played by Big Dan Foulkes in 'The Deal'

Scotty Cameron Newport 2 putter (a snip at £329). Argent Brierley requested one in 'The Boy's Champion' – but he still lost the putting competition.

A GEM putter as used by the Jock in 'My Golfing Romance'.

E R Whitcombe Mashie or 5 Iron, as used by The Duke in 'The Thirties Man'. Inherited and used by Jock.

Ben Sayers Crown forged Iron. As used by Jock's father in 'Play Golf Not War'

A George Lowe putter, as used by Jock in 'Play Golf not war'. It was part of Jock Romanes set which was inherited by Jock's dad

The Mills mallet headed putter. Part of Jock's unmatched first set of clubs - 'The Golf club O-holic'

George Nicoll Pinsplitter iron – The Author still has a set

Ben Sayers 'Dreadnought' driver. As quoted in 'Play Golf not War'

Benross Compressor Iron. Currently occupying the Author's golf bag

A Nicoll 'Howitzer' sand wedge, part of Jock Romanes set which was inherited by Jock's dad – 'Play Golf not War'

A 1990 Mizuno 4 Iron, as used by the Author in 'People I have met on the golf course' (versus D Haddow)

Bronze Ping Anser putter, as used by Jimmy Gibb in 'The Boy's Champion'

A Ben Sayers 'Special' putter, part of Jock's Dad's matched set, assembled gradually during the mid to late 1930's.

The Bridge of Weir Leather Co, where Kinghorn 'tacky' grips were made – Jock's dad's club grips – 'Play Golf not War'

MacGregor irons as used by Jack Nicklaus to win the 1986 Masters. The 1960's versions were used by Jock Romanes in 'Play Golf not War'

A Titleist DCI Copy iron. One of a set of 'Knock off' clubs purchased by the Author in the mid 1990's

Lynx BlackCat iron. Played by Fred Couples in the 1990's 'Golf Club O-holic'

Ping 3 Wood TISI Tec Titanium – played in the 2000's by Miguel Angel Jimenez 'Golf Club O-holic'

Ping Eye 2 laminated 3 wood 'Golf Club O-holic' and 'The Boys Champion'

Ping Zero putter, still in the Author's collection - 'Golf Club O-holic'

Willie Kidd backwards putter, circa 1910. 'My favourite Golf Books' – ref. David Graham)

Cars featuring in the Book.

The Author, while not professing to be a petrolhead, nevertheless has missed no opportunity to include cars of various sorts in his stories. The following are a few, with references to their location in the book.

The Squire Sports car 1936 – only seven ever manufactured (The Thirties Man)

1968 Blue Morris Minor (The Boys Champion)

Pink Cadillac Eldorado (The Boys Champion)

British Racing Green MGB GT with silver Minilite wheels (Close Encounter)

Big Dan's Audi A8. (The Deal)

Ms Lascelles new Mazda MX 5 sports car (The Thirties Man)

*1998 Ford Focus – Ms
Jenny Hinton (Play Golf
not war)*

*1966 Ford Mustang
Convertible
(Play Golf not war)*

*1985 Ford Escort
(Characters I have met on
the golf course – Ronnie
Simpson)*

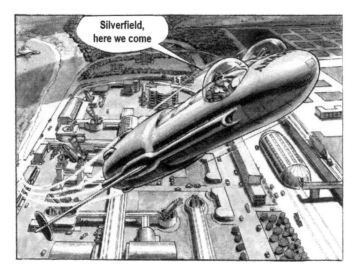

Unidentified vehicle (Close Encounter)

In Memoriam, Argent Brierley, 1893-1960

Cramond - 1914

Figures in a park - 1914

Bank Holiday 1940